EVERY STUDENT
SUCCEEDS

A CONCEPTUAL FRAMEWORK FOR STUDENTS AT RISK OF SCHOOL FAILURE

*An initiative jointly sponsored by
the California State Board of Education
and the California Department of Education*

PUBLISHING INFORMATION

Every Student Succeeds: A Conceptual Framework for Students At Risk of School Failure was developed by the California State Board of Education and the California Department of Education with the guidance and assistance of the many individuals listed in the acknowledgments. Dennis Parker was the principal author of the document. The document was prepared and initially published by Resources in Special Education (RiSE), a special project of California State University, Sacramento, through an interagency agreement with the California Department of Education (No. 2297). It was edited for publication by Patricia Winget, Manager, and Elissa Cullison, Associate Editor, RiSE. Design and layout of the document were created by Sandra Cosner, Graphic Artist, and Frances Baca, Graphic Designer, RiSE.

The document was published by the California Department of Education, 721 Capitol Mall, Sacramento, California (mailing address: P.O. Box 944272, Sacramento, CA 94244-2720).

ISBN 0-8011-1177-3

Copies of *Every Student Succeeds* are available for $11.75 each, plus sales tax for California residents, from the Bureau of Publications, Sales Unit, California Department of Education, P.O. Box 271, Sacramento, CA 95812-0271. A catalog and supplement describing other educational resources available from the Department can be obtained by writing to the address above or by calling the Sales Unit at 916/445-1260.

Contents

EVERY STUDENT SUCCEEDS

FOREWORD

Although we have made substantial progress in improving California's educational system during the past 12 years, we have been seriously challenged to ensure that all students succeed in their current elementary or secondary education and are prepared for the future job market and our changing society. The California State Board of Education and the California Department of Education addressed this challenge during our December 1989 California Education Summit and as a result created the Every Student Succeeds (ESS) initiative.

The spirit of the initiative was set in the spring of 1990 when Bill Honig, State Superintendent of Public Instruction, Ed Foglia, California Teachers Association President, Mary Standlee, President of the California School Boards Association, and two outstanding superintendents, Robert Flores from Alisal Union Elementary School District and Rudy Castruita from Santa Ana Unified School District, spoke to district teams in Oakland and Los Angeles. The State leaders committed their organizations to work together and support local districts which were willing to have educators, parents, and community members work together to promote the best educational, psychological, and social experience possible for every student — especially those students who are at risk of school failure. In 1991, 10 school districts and 46 schools agreed to accept this challenge. This conceptual framework represents the best thinking about educating every student and has been developed and implemented in part by the schools and districts participating in this initiative.

This initiative is consistent with the Department's four age-span publications and initiatives: *Here They Come, Ready or Not*; *It's Elementary*; *Caught in the Middle*; and *Second to None*. It is also consistent with the school restructuring legislation under S.B. 1274 and the Healthy Start Program legislation under S.B. 620. We also believe it is consistent with federal legislation: Goals 2000, the National and Community Service Trust Act, the School to Work Transition Act, and the Improving America's Schools Act.

The California State Board of Education and the California Department of Education invite all districts and schools to consider joining this initiative to create an integrated, coherent, comprehensive education system that will result in success for every student.

MARION MCDOWELL
President, California State Board of Education

WILLIAM D. DAWSON
Acting State Superintendent of Public Instruction

EVERY STUDENT SUCCEEDS

PREFACE

The Every Student Succeeds (ESS) initiative has grown and developed with much spirit but few funds. We are indebted to the many individuals who have participated in the development, implementation, and evaluation of the Every Student Succeeds (ESS) initiative. Bill Honig, former State Superintendent, lit the ESS flame during the December 1989 Education Summit by creating a group to make recommendations about students at risk of school failure. Rudy Crew, former Sacramento City Unified School District Superintendent, led the group of approximately 40 Summit participants who studied the research and practice regarding students at risk of school failure and recommended that an initiative be created to address the needs of these students more effectively and to use State and Federal categorical program funding more effectively to that end.

An external advisory group consisting of the individuals listed in the Acknowledgments Section provided the advice to the California Department of Education (CDE) staff group in developing the January 1991 *ESS Working Draft* as the precursor to this paper. Dennis Parker acted as primary writer of that paper and incorporated the comments of the external group as well as the CDE staff listed in the Acknowledgments Section.

A summary of the *Working Draft* inviting school and district teams to participate in this initiative, was sent to all California schools and districts as part of the S.B. 1274 School Restructuring Briefing Papers in April 1990. Thus, schools and districts were given the opportunity to apply to join either or both initiatives.

Approximately 400 of the 1,400 S.B. 1274 applicant schools wrote restructuring planning grants and indicated they were interested in participating in the ESS initiative. An additional, special review of these planning grants resulted in teams of CDE staff paired with external advisory group members ultimately selecting ten ESS districts and 46 schools. The local boards, administrators, teachers, parents, and community members in the ESS schools and districts agreed to waive provisions of their most cherished directives (e.g., district policies, teacher union agreements, etc.) when specific provisions got in the way of achieving every student's success. The State agreed to provide support by assisting with State Board waivers and responding to collective and individual school and district requests.

The ESS districts and schools have held five networking meetings to date (see Appendix B for a summary of these meetings), and many of these schools and districts have demonstrated an uncommon commitment to teaching every student effectively. As a result of these network meetings and CDE staff input, the *ESS Working Draft* has become the *ESS Conceptual Framework*. Although the two goals and six major elements have remained similar during this evolutionary period, we have noted three critical changes. The first is that those persons responsible for students' success must really believe that every student *can* succeed. We noted that approximately 80 percent of the teachers were white and middle-class but were teaching students who were generally children of color from a different social class. This presented a critical barrier to student success. Although teachers cannot change their ethnicity or socioeconomic backgrounds, they can develop beliefs in the potential of success of every child and they can develop their ability to teach all children effectively. Dr. Jeff Howard from the Efficacy Institute and his staff have challenged the ESS participants during two network meetings to work systematically through those issues which prevent them from providing a truly world class education for poor, minority group, and special needs students.

The second change in the initiative has manifested itself in Element Three of the conceptual framework: "An integrated program — with a personal touch." Research on "resilient students" and observations of students succeeding who were at risk of not succeeding show that a caring adult believed in, supported, and mentored the student. Thus, merely setting up effective institutional systems seemed to be necessary but not sufficient for student success. A personal relationship with every student over a sustained period of time is critical.

Finally, Element Six, "Whatever Else It Takes," has taken on concrete meaning within the ESS Network. It starts with a group of people being honestly critical of the effects of their instructional strategies when they note that not every student is succeeding. In Paramount Elementary School in Azusa Unified School District, a single elementary school teacher volunteered to take all primary grade students in her school who were artistic, kinesthetic learners and to teach these students in a multigrade situation for a year. The teachers union was convinced to waive its prohibition in the collective bargaining agreement against multi-grade assignments so that the teacher could try her experiment. After one year, almost all of her students could read well enough to succeed in the regular classrooms.

In another ESS example, Almeria Middle School in Fontana Unified School District, which was generally achieving exceptional results, acknowledged that approximately 100 of its sixth, seventh, and eighth graders were "falling through the cracks." They created a special four-week summer course which included a potpourri of activities: ropes courses to enhance self-esteem, tutoring programs to assist students master subjects in which they felt weak, electronic portfolios for assessment, and other strategies. The result has been dramatic; most of these students are back on track to graduate successfully from this middle school.

We are not, however, allowing anecdotes to determine the success of this initiative. We have enlisted the assistance of Far West Laboratory in San Francisco to evaluate it. They will soon be publishing ten school case studies and a synthesis of learning about these schools, which will provide an empirical basis for assisting other schools.

Thus, the purpose of this publication is to provide a conceptual framework for educators, parents, and community members at the state, district, and school levels who are interested in restructuring and reforming their educational and related programs to ensure that every student succeeds. The journey to ensuring every student's success is long, but a significant number of people have committed to it and have been transformed in the process.

WADE BRYNELSON
Assistant Superintendent/ESS Manager

MARGARET FORTUNE
ESS Coordinator

DENNIS PARKER
Manager, Language Arts and Foreign Languages Office

ACKNOWLEDGMENTS

Every Student Succeeds: A Conceptual Framework for Students At Risk of School Failure is the result of an active partnership between the California Department of Education (CDE), the State Board of Education, school districts, school sites, and a variety of public and private agencies. The development of this framework represents a comprehensive collaboration among educators involved in working with children who are at risk of school failure presently or who may be at risk in the future.

Many educators contributed to the original development of the ESS initiative in 1991 and to the continuously evolving efforts. These educators gave generously of their time at planning and networking meetings, while many others made revisions and additions to the conceptual framework, which was approved by the Department's Executive Committee and the State Board of Education. We would like to give special appreciation to the following individuals:

For their early work with the ESS initiative beginning in 1991,

the EVERY STUDENT SUCCEEDS EXTERNAL ADVISORY COMMITTEE:

CHARLES ACOSTA
*Past President, California Association
of Bilingual Educators*

BARBARA ALEXANDER
*Past President, Western Coalition
of Title I/Chapter 1 Parents*

LINDA BOURGAIZE
Past President, SELPA Directors

ANASTACIO CABRAL
*Principal, Frank Paul Elementary
Alisal Union Elementary School District*

JOYA CHATTERJEE
*Principal, Westwood Elementary
Santa Clara Unified School District*

WILLIAM J. CIRONE
*Santa Barbara County Superintendent of Schools
Association of County Superintendents*

PHIL DARO
*Director, New Standards Project
University of California, Office of the President*

PAT DINGSDALE
Vice President, Parent Teachers Association

KATHRYN DRONENBURG
Member, State Board of Education

AMY DUNCAN
*Past President, California Association
of Program Specialists*

BILL EWING
*Director, Child Development
Pomona Unified School District*

LYNN FOX
*Professor of Education, Special Education
San Francisco State University*

MARLYN FRANKLIN
*California Teachers Association Representative
Adams School, Redondo Beach City
School District*

HELEN FRIED
*Former Director of Education Services,
ABC Unified School District*

JERROLD FRYE
*Past President, California Association of
Administrators of State and Federal
Education Programs*

TOM GIUGNI
*Executive Director, Association of California
School Administrators*

MARY ANN GOLEMBESKY
*Past President, Learning Disability
Association of California*

LARRY GUTHRIE
Guthrie Associates, San Francisco

CALVIN HALL
*Past President, California Association
of School Business Officers*

VICTORIA JEW
*Past President, California Association
for Asian-Pacific Bilingual Education*

ANN KINKOR
*Past President, Advisory Commission
on Special Education*

CONNIE LAPIN
Special Education Reform Advisory Committee

RUTH MCKENNA
*Associate Superintendent, Instruction
New Haven Unified School District*

STEVEN MINJAREZ
*Director, Pupil Personnel and Special Services
Galeta Union Elementary School District*

WAYNE MIYAMOTO
*Executive Director, California Association
of Private Specialized Education*

TIM MURPHY
*Consultant in Charge, Curriculum Programs
and Instructional Technologies
Los Angeles County Office of Education*

PAUL NAVA
*Director, Migrant Education
Pajaro Valley Unified School District*

SUSANA NAVARRO
Former Executive Director, Achievement Council

ELIZABETH NORWOOD
*Public Information Officer, C-LERN
Inglewood Unified School District*

KENT PAXTON
*Network Officer, City and County Interagency
Children's Services Network*

CHUCK PILLSBURY
Program Review Analyst, Department of Finance

JOE PLATOW
*Former Chief Executive Officer,
California Association of School Psychologists*

BARBARA RAO
*Board of Directors, California School
Employees Association*

RAY REINHART
*Assistant Secretary, Office of Child Development
and Education*

JUDY ROSEBERRY
Past President, California Association for the Gifted

TOM RUIZ
*Former Program Coordinator for Restructuring,
San Francisco Unified School District*

DR. WAYNE SAILOR
*Professor, University of Kansas
The Association for the Severely Handicapped*

MARIE SCHRUP
Consultant, Commission on Teacher Credentialing

RICK SIMPSON
*Education Consultant to Speaker of the
California Assembly*

STEVEN SLOAN
*Past President, California Teachers of English to
Speakers of Other Languages*

VELMA STRONG
Past President, Coalition of Chapter 1 Parents

JOAN TROPPMANN
*Past President, California Association
of Resource Specialists*

CHARITY WEBB
Past President, California School Boards Association

For their continuous work with the initiative, the California Department of Education's (CDE) EVERY STUDENT SUCCEEDS ADVISORY COMMITTEE, which also includes non-CDE staff:

JOE BARANKIN
Supervising Field Representative,
Education Finance Division

BARBARA BASEGGIO
Manager, Elementary Education Unit,
Curriculum, Instruction, and Assessment Division

LYNN BAUGHER
Manager, Consolidated Programs and Information
Management, Compliance and Consolidated
Programs Division

PETER BIRDSALL
President, Peter Birdsall and Associates

BARBARA BRANDES
Manager, High School Education Office, Instruc-
tional Services and Teaching Support Division

CHARLOTTE CAMERON
Staff Service Analyst, CalServe/ESS, Compliance
and Consolidated Programs Division

SUSAN COX
Office Technician, CalServe/ESS, Compliance
and Consolidated Programs Division

PAMELA DAVIS
Manager, Liaison Office to the Commission
on Teacher Credentialing, Instructional Services
and Teaching Support Division

JANICE DeBENEDETTI
Manager, Home Economics Education, Career
and Vocational Education Division

THADDEUS DUMAS
Assistant Superintendent/Director, Instructional
Services and Teaching Support Division

BOB EVANS
Manager, School Interventions and Educational
Options Unit, Youth, Adult, and Alternative
Educational Services Division

LINDA FORSYTH
Executive Director, California Commission
for Improving Life Through Service

SUANNA GILMAN-PONCE
Consultant, Complaints Management and
Bilingual Compliance Unit, Compliance and
Consolidated Programs Division

CONNIE GIPSON
Vocational Education Gender Equality Consultant,
Career-Vocational Education Division

LUCILLE GONZALES
Consultant, Regional Programs and
Special Projects Division

DAVID GORDON
Former Deputy Superintendent, Program
Assistance and Compliance Branch

SHELLEY HARRIS
Consultant, Program, Curriculum and Training,
Special Education Division

WENDY HARRIS
Manager, Office of School Improvement,
Regional Programs and Special Projects Division

LYNN HARTZLER
Consultant, School Intervention and
Educational Options,Youth, Adult, and
Alternative Educational Services Division

JANE HENDERSON
Director, Interagency Children and Youth
Services Division

AMY HIBBITT
Office Technician, Education Finance Division

JO ANN IZU
Project Director, Far West Laboratory, San Francisco

RON KADISH
Superintendent
State Special Schools and Services Division

DON KAIROTT
Consultant, Elementary Education Office,
Curriculum, Instruction, and Assessment Division

JUDITH KINGSLEY
Former Deputy Superintendent,
Program Assistance and Service Coordination Branch

KAREN LOWREY
Consultant, CLAS,
Curriculum, Instruction, and Assessment Division

DAVE PATTERSON
Consultant, Regional Programs and
Special Projects Division

VIRGINIA REYNOLDS
Educational Systems and Services Consultant,
California State University, Sacramento

SUSAN THOMPSON
Manager, Management Planning and Special
Projects Unit, Child Development Division

MERRILL VARGO
Director, Regional Programs and
Special Projects Division

JON ILITA WHITE
Consultant and Special Assistant,
Categorical Programs Division

SALLIE WILSON
Consultant, Office of Compensatory
Education, Categorical Programs Division

PAT WINGET
Program Manager
Resources in Special Education (RiSE)

LORNA WINTER
Consultant, Regional Programs
and Special Projects Division

For their continuous work as liaisons between the participating districts, school sites,
and the Department of Education, the EVERY STUDENT SUCCEEDS DISTRICT REPRESENTATIVES:

LINDA DELGUIDICE
Coordinator, Student Achievement Program,
Santa Ana Unified School District

STEVE FISH
Deputy Superintendent
Long Beach Joint Unified School District

MARLIN FOXWORTH
Superintendent
Hayward Unified School District

MAX HARRELL
Director, Educational Services, Dos Palos
Oro Loma Joint Unified School District

KAREN HARSHMAN
Superintendent
Fontana Unified School District

JEANNE HERRICK
Director, Bilingual Education,
Alisal Union School District

WILMA KOZAI
Principal, Carver Elementary School,
San Diego Unified School District

NANCY MOORE
Assistant Superintendent, Educational
Services, Azusa Unified School District

BERT POST
Assistant Superintendent
Secondary Education
Pajaro Valley Unified School District

RAYMOND VALDEZ
Principal, Fern Bacon Middle School,
Sacramento City Unified School District

EDUCATION IS
EVERYONE'S
BUSINESS

*"Social welfare programs may be
a matter of ethics and generosity,
but education and training are not. I am willing
to pay for, indeed insist upon, the education
of my neighbors' children not because I am
generous but because I cannot afford to live
with them undereducated. "*

LESTER C. THUROW, ECONOMIST
Cited in *The Forgotten Half*, November, 1988
The William T. Grant Foundation, Washington, D.C.

EVERY STUDENT SUCCEEDS

INTRODUCTION

The purpose of this manual is to provide a conceptual framework guiding the policies and intervention strategies of schools for students at risk. The central premise is that it is possible to help virtually every child learn a district's core curriculum at acceptable levels of proficiency. The framework presented here will, it is hoped, improve schooling for all students, even for the most gifted or talented. What is best for the least successful students will also improve schooling for the best. This focus will ultimately lead to programs that will help every student become a competent adult and effective citizen of the twenty-first century.

As used in this initiative, the term *student at risk* refers broadly to any student with whom the school is not now succeeding or to any student who appears susceptible to having problems in school in the near future. The ESS initiative addresses any range of concentrations of these students — from isolated individuals in an otherwise successful school to a majority of the population at a low-performing school. The framework provided in this paper can help schools organize themselves to be more successful with all of their students. Ultimately, however, each school community must determine for itself which of its students are at risk and develop its own versions of programs and services to support every student's success.

— *Lathrop Intermediate School, Santa Ana Unified School District*

It is possible to help virtually every child learn a district's core curriculum at acceptable levels of proficiency.

ESS

The ESS initiative includes the ideas of many individuals and groups in the Department and in the field. It also incorporates key elements of a number of proposals for the reform of categorical programs, including:

◆ Special education
◆ Previous and current proposals and programs to improve low-performing schools
◆ The School Improvement Program (SIP) model for planning and implementing change
◆ The School-Based Coordination Program (SBCP)
◆ Chapter 1 Program Improvement
◆ The Continuous Quality Improvement Schools Program
◆ The work of the Achievement Council
◆ The integrated program items in the Department of Education's *Coordinated Compliance Review Manual*
◆ The curriculum frameworks adopted by the State Board of Education
◆ The California School Leadership Academy's training materials
◆ Other state publications (such as *Here They Come: Ready or Not, It's Elementary, Caught in the Middle,* and *Second to None*)
◆ The professional literature on school change, students at risk, early childhood development, and cognitive psychology
◆ Career-Vocational education

Teachers and students work one-on-one at Almeria Middle School in the Fontana Unified School District.

Also reflected is input from many colleagues in the field who are familiar with and in some cases are operating successful programs for students at risk, including the ESS demonstration schools and districts. From the beginning key ideas and priorities from the California Education Summit (December 1989) and major California educational organizations have guided this work. All of these ideas were built into the Every Student Succeeds *Working Paper* (January, 1991). This 1994 publication is an extension and refinement of that first work and has been enriched by continual comments from Department staff and from educators in the field dedicated to this effort. In short, Every Student Succeeds builds on the best thinking of many to provide a current conceptual framework that schools and school districts may draw upon to enhance their capacities for success with students at risk.

THE SIX GUIDING ELEMENTS

Six guiding elements make up this framework. The first two are major goals, and the remaining four are strategies to accomplish those goals.

MAJOR GOALS

1. Organize and operate schools so that every student succeeds in learning the district's rich core curriculum through effective instruction as described in the state frameworks and in a manner responsive to individual and group strengths, needs, interests, and learning characteristics. Success should be determined by student outcomes and not by mere exposure to the curriculum or the opportunity to learn. This effort requires every member of the school community — staff, parents, and community members — to believe in and actively support each student's success.

2. Identify students at risk of failure early. At the first sign of difficulty, intervene to prevent failure in the future by building on strengths through enrichment rather than by compensating for deficits through remediation. Whatever remediation is offered should be early, intensive, effective, and short-lived.

IMPLEMENTATION STRATEGIES

3. Integrate all core and supplementary services for each student. To be included are services provided through categorical programs, special education services provided by school and school district auxiliary personnel, and services provided by health and social service agencies. By this action students can be ensured the most effective, comprehensive, integrated, and coherent educational experience possible. All of this effort should be made with the support and involvement of parents and community members and should include at least one caring relationship between each student and an adult.

4. Provide effective learning experiences for staff, parents, and community members on topics related to the other five guiding elements in this framework and focus on enhancing student achievement. Sufficient follow-up to training, such as coaching, monitoring, and establishing collegial support groups, should be provided to ensure full implementation.

5. Establish school site processes and structures to plan, implement, and evaluate initiatives to improve dramatically the school's effect on the optimal academic, psychological, and social development of its students at risk both individually and collectively. Making time to carry out this component is crucial to the success of whatever is attempted.

6. Do whatever else it takes — within legal, professional, and ethical standards — to enable every student, by name, to succeed in school academically, psychologically, and socially — no matter what. The ongoing concern, good will, and ingenuity of people working with students and schools will ultimately make the difference for the most vulnerable students.

ELEMENT 1:
Success in Learning
a Rich Core Curriculum

ELEMENT 2:
A Preventive Approach

ELEMENT 3:
Integrated Total Program
for Each Student,
with a Personal Touch

ELEMENT 4
Effective Staff
Development

ELEMENT 5:
Planning,
Implementing,
and Evaluating

ELEMENT 6:
Whatever Else It Takes

CONTEXT OF *ESS* IMPLEMENTATION

1. *Schools without an operating change model*

2. *Schools with one operating change model*

3. *Schools with many operating change models*

IMPLEMENTING THE INITIATIVE

Now faced with education's most demanding challenge — to achieve success with every child in an increasingly diverse student population — educators must generate a variety of solutions to problems within and outside the school. Regardless of the value of experimentation and creativity in this effort, it is important to base practice on a set of solid values and sound educational research. This framework attempts to establish the basis for innovative practices by addressing both. Any model developed for students at risk should address all of the elements of this conceptual framework, and educators concerned about students at risk should guide their efforts accordingly.

This initiative might be implemented in three settings. The first is a school that lacks a schoolwide model for change in operations. In this case the six-point framework and supporting material might serve as a model for uniting the school community in a comprehensive effort to improve its ability to succeed with students at risk.

The second setting is a school that already has a unifying schoolwide project in operation, such as the Continuous Quality Improvement Schools Program, School Restructuring (S.B. 1274), the Achievement Council, Chapter 1 Program Improvement, the James Comer Model, Ted Sizer's Coalition of Essential Schools, Robert Slavin's Success for All Program, or Henry Levin's Accelerated Schools Program. In this case following the tenets of ESS might facilitate a more comprehensive or balanced version of the current program. However, the existing schoolwide approach does not have to be replaced by ESS. Rather, it should operate according to whatever model the school has been using.

The third setting involves a school that may have as many as three or four schoolwide change models operating simultaneously (e.g., the School Improvement Program, the Achievement Council, and a Chapter 1 schoolwide project). In this case ESS could unify the various programs and models, perhaps serving as the vehicle by which the school community might establish a division of labor among the various models and thereby coordinate their implementation.

Currently a total of 49 ESS demonstration schools (K–12) are operating in ten school districts. Fourteen of those schools have received grants for restructuring under Senate Bill 1274. In addition, a number of other schools and districts, together with the Department and the ESS schools and districts, are participating in an interactive information-sharing network. But this is just the beginning. If every student is to succeed, schools across the state need to make the commitment and begin the strategies embodied in this initiative. ☙

BACKGROUND AND FOCUS OF THIS INITIATIVE

CONDITIONS IN CALIFORNIA SCHOOLS

Recognizing the effects of such negative health and social conditions as substance abuse, gang membership and negative peer pressure, poverty, poor diet, and changing family structures, the California Department of Education, the State Board of Education, and participating ESS districts and schools are supporting the Every Student Succeeds initiative to improve educational outcomes for all California students significantly.

Staggering statistics representing the current conditions affecting children in California have prompted this united effort.

◆ 1 of 2 California children will live in a single-parent household by age eighteen (*Children Now*, 1994).

◆ 1 of 3 California children is born to an unmarried mother (Alan Guttmacher Institute, 1994).

◆ 34.2% of California public school students are language-minority students (CDE Demographics Unit, 1993).

◆ 22.2% of the students enrolled in California schools are limited-English proficient (CDE Demographics Unit, 1993).

◆ 18.2 % of California school children lived in poverty in 1989 (*Children Now*, 1994).

◆ California has the highest teenage pregnancy rate in the nation for those fifteen through nineteen years of age (Alan Guttmacher Institute, 1994).

◆ California must find space and materials for approximately 100,000 additional students each year for the next ten years (CDE Demographics Unit, 1994).

As a result of these and other unprecedented political and economic challenges to California's schools, too many children are failing or are at risk of failing in school. However, California's dropout rate fell from 25 percent in 1986 to 16.6 percent in 1992. Unfortunately, the high rates for Hispanics (24.6 percent) and African Americans (26.4 percent) are still unacceptably disproportionate to the rates for Asians (9.2 percent) and whites (10.8 percent) (California Department of Education, 1993-94). In some districts the dropout rate may exceed 50 percent, especially for students who are migrant or who are culturally/linguistically diverse. This dropout rate also represents students who may be learning disabled or who are from low income families.

Performance on state and national norm-referenced tests also reflects disproportionately low scores in addition to disproportionately low rates of enrollment in and graduation from college for these same groups. Moreover, the results of the *Scholastic Aptitude Test* — in spite of gains for all groups in recent years — continue to reflect significant and consistent gaps between the scores achieved by minority students, such as African Americans, American Indians, and Hispanics, and the scores achieved by white students. And the results involve only the better students.

Although many of the conditions described previously are beyond the power of educators to change, several critical conditions, practices, or educational structures within schools can and should be improved immediately. For example, many of the lowest-performing schools tend to have a curriculum almost exclusively skills-based and intrinsically uninteresting to students at risk. And such schools often use instructional strategies that do not help the lowest-performing students interact intensely with the curriculum. Moreover, even high-performing schools that may have better curricula and instructional practices often do not offer these advantages to students viewed as underachieving or at risk. In short, in some schools an effective educational program is unavailable; in others it is available but not to all students. A good source of guidance for developing more powerful curricula and instructional strategies for all students can be found in California's curriculum frameworks.

STUMBLING BLOCKS

Probably the single most important school structure blocking many students' access to a district's core curriculum is homogeneous ability grouping or tracking. Schools can immediately begin to study alternative grouping patterns and seriously consider the use of a more effective variety of configurations based on student interests, language backgrounds, proficiency in English, strengths, curricular themes, student projects, and so forth.

A second obstacle is an overreliance on a skills-based curriculum. Organizing instruction around a sequence of facts and skills, abstracted from the real world, often results in a meaningless and trivialized educational experience for many students. Such a curriculum also lends itself to the most damaging kinds of homogeneous grouping for low

Students work together on a science project at Azusa High School, Azusa Unified School District.

achievers. And it frequently leads to positioning the most meaningful and interesting parts of the curriculum until the "basics" have been mastered first. Unfortunately, some students find themselves working on basic skills and facts their entire school career.

A third stumbling block involves testing. Many student assessment practices and the kinds of data most often reported tend to shape and sustain a skills-based curriculum, a teacher-centered transmission model of instruction, and a deficit belief system in relation to certain groups of students. Existing tests indicate two kinds of problems. On the one hand students have been tested to determine their needs (i.e., their weaknesses or deficits) in order to place them, traditionally, in a high, middle, or low track. On the other hand many, if not most, of the limited-English-proficient students in the state are not systematically tested at all, even in their primary language, when instruction is provided in that language (*CDE Compliance Streamlining Committee's Report*, 1992).

When new and better accountability measures are developed and put into practice, teachers are able to shift to a more meaning-centered, interactive, and enrichment model of curriculum and more instruction. And when assessment information is used to identify and advocate for student strengths and interests rather than highlight and legitimize their weaknesses or shortcomings, underachieving students will be empowered rather than systematically disabled (Cummins, 1986).

When assessment information is used to identify and advocate for student strengths and interests rather than highlight and legitimize their weaknesses or shortcomings, underachieving students will be empowered rather than systematically disabled.

A student learns to read at West Randall Elementary School, Azusa Unified School District.

A fourth major area of immediate exploration for schools in trouble with students at risk is the coordination of the total school program for each student. Often, the coordination of services and the close collaboration of adults working with the same multifunded students are lacking. This lack of coordination is often present at the school, school district, county, and state levels. The traditional requirements of fiscal accountability by funding source are most often cited as reasons for what may easily become a fragmented program from the student's point of view. Policies for tracking expenditures have often prevented specialists supported by different funding sources from formally sharing their expertise, planning collaboratively, or coordinating their efforts with each other and with classroom teachers. Being able to coordinate funds and personnel efficiently and maintain safeguards for the students for whom the funds are intended is a challenge for staffs trying to have a more effective impact on the academic success of multifunded students. School-based coordination programs (SBCP) for state categorical funds and Elementary and Secondary Education Act (ESEA), Chapter 1, schoolwide projects offer many flexibilities and possibilities for coordinating funding.

Finally, although historically difficult to accomplish, the coordination of health and social services at school for children and parents in need is beginning to win acceptance in many school communities. Better access to such services by brokering them on campus can immediately remove many obstacles for parents and subsequently support opportunities for their children to do their best academically. Such services might address such problems as neglect, inadequate diet, poor hygiene, physical and emotional abuse, substance abuse, poverty, homelessness, poor attendance, and cognitive and emotional disabilities, including those related to the effects of drugs before or after birth. The Healthy Start statewide grant program, currently in planning or operation in 930 schools, gives schools, in partnership with public and private service providers, the opportunity to make available comprehensive support services for children and their families. Services range from academic support services to health, mental health, social, and family support services.

IMPORTANCE OF STAFF DEVELOPMENT

The Every Student Succeeds initiative is built on the fundamental belief that every student, given the proper program, will succeed in school. Yet educators working with the lowest-performing students often develop a low sense of efficacy or lack of confidence in their ability to succeed with these students. They may also lack the conviction that such students can succeed academically. That attitude is understandable in view of (1) the traditional interpretation of such background factors as socioeconomic status, parent education level, and ethnicity as explanations or causes of low performance rather than as mere statistical correlates; (2) the daily reality of the students' poor performance; and (3) the frequent lack of resources and time to research and implement remedies that could significantly change the status quo.

Staff development that arms educators with new and more effective practices, a supportive school culture, and the subsequent achievement of positive results with local students can promote the positive sense of efficacy necessary to sustain high levels of performance by adults and students in a school system (McLaughlin & Marsh, 1978; Howard, 1993).

A word of caution is in order, however, especially for the most zealous of educational reformers. Schools that are the most sensitive to students' problems and the most willing to incorporate all of the current reforms into their programs may easily become overwhelmed, overextended, and pulled in many directions at once. The result is a loss of impact on students and confusion, disillusion, and burnout for the staff. Research on school change, on the other hand, indicates that if a school can unify its efforts around a single vision of academic success for every student and progressively implement a limited number of ambitious initiatives for change, then dramatic, positive results are inevitable.

GOALS AND FOCUS OF THE INITIATIVE

The Every Student Succeeds initiative has two major goals. The first goal is to ensure that every student learns a rich, meaning-centered core curriculum. Many schools, therefore, must improve dramatically the achievement of students who are failing or are at risk of failing. The second major goal is to establish a preventive approach to schooling, focusing on helping each student avoid or solve any problem that might impede his or her optimal development — academically, psychologically, or socially.

> *Staff development that arms educators with new and more effective practices, a supportive school culture, and the subsequent achievement of positive results with local students can promote the positive sense of efficacy necessary to sustain high levels of performance by adults and students in a school system.*

INVOLVEMENT OF ALL STUDENTS

The scope of this initiative is *all students* receiving publicly funded programs and services in preschool through grade twelve. Within this focus problems and successes can be considered from several points of view. For example, one approach is to look at the school's entire student population. This was the approach taken initially by the effective schools movement in the early to mid-eighties. Schoolwide measures, such as test scores, attendance, grades, dropout rates, or college-enrollment rates were used as indices of a school's overall effectiveness. Although still useful and recommended here, this approach has been found to be flawed, especially when used as the *only* approach to improving school- ing for *all* students. For example, a large school could get high marks for its schoolwide averages that mask the failure of sizable segments of its population (e.g., its Chapter 1 or limited-English-proficient students). Thus, looking at students from the point of view of a schoolwide average may be one important focus but is insufficient for validating every student's success.

FOCUS ON STUDENT OUTCOMES

A second approach is to look at the outcomes for each group of stu- dents served by a categorical program, such as those served by the school's bilingual, compensatory, migrant, vocational, gifted and talented, or special education programs. Variations in outcomes by gender can also be included to determine, for example, how females compare with males in mathemat- ics and science. One might also look at outcomes by ethnic group to deter- mine what proportion of whites, Hispanics, African Americans, Asians, American Indians, or others are winning academic awards, participating in school and community programs outside of the classroom, scoring high on tests, taking college preparatory courses, choosing to major in the humani- ties and social sciences as well as mathematics and science, attending school regularly or dropping out, and so forth.

Interestingly, this student population approach represents a new level of refinement that has now been incorporated into today's versions of the effective schools model whereby schools are being encouraged to disaggregate their data by student population. This perspective better illuminates the effect the school is having on *all* of its students. The goals of excellence *and* equity can no longer be discussed without looking at student populations in this way. However, neither the schoolwide view nor the approach by student populations will necessarily reveal how a school is doing with every student and what might be done to ensure each one's success.

STUDENT ACHIEVEMENT AND DEVELOPMENT

A third perspective, therefore, is to focus on both the individual student's academic achievement and psychological and social development. When outcomes are viewed in this way, students at risk include children who (1) are doing fine now but who — because of particular home, community, or school circumstances — may be susceptible to academic, psychological, or social problems in the future; and (2) are already manifesting problems in these areas. Such problems might never be revealed and consequently never addressed if only the schoolwide or group perspectives discussed previously are employed. Examples of concerns at this more idiosyncratic level include but are not limited to signs of alienation or disengagement from school, emotional or behavioral problems, poor health and nutrition, pregnancy, neglect, physical or emotional abuse, substance abuse, homelessness, war trauma, culture shock, financial problems, negative peer pressure, low career aspirations, low self-esteem, and delinquency.

In the final analysis the school community must be willing to address such concerns and do whatever it takes to succeed on three fronts: schoolwide, with each student population, and, ultimately, with each student.

PREMISES UNDERLYING THE INITIATIVE

Several premises underlie the Every Student Succeeds initiative. Although not new, they are often difficult to put into practice, especially for students at risk — a matter of crucial importance.

STUDENTS AT RISK CAN SUCCEED

The first premise is the belief that students at risk can do as well in school as other students — in spite of any factors, predictors, or outcome data to the contrary. There are schools that have, in spite of obstacles, demonstrated success with students at risk. For example, the California distinguished schools awards are given on a competitive basis to outstanding schools that have high or improving test scores and pass an on-site review of a team of evaluators. Twenty-five of the 1987 winners were schools composed of at least 60 percent combined Hispanic and African-American populations, many in communities that are largely poor. Awards are given every year by the Department of Education to achieving compensatory education schools. Nationally recognized models that have also proven to be dramatically successful with students at risk include those developed by James Comer, Henry Levin, and

The school community must be willing to address such concerns and do whatever it takes to succeed on three fronts: schoolwide, with each student population, and, ultimately, with each student.

Students pan for gold during "Gold Rush Days" at Paramount Elementary School, Azusa Unified School District.

Robert Slavin; the Bilingual Case Studies and Two-Way Bilingual models in California; the Santa Fe Indian School; the Benjamin E. Mays Academy in Atlanta; Debbie Meier's Central Park East Secondary School in Harlem; and the Coca-Cola Youth Partnership Program in San Antonio. See also George Wood's *Schools That Work* (1992) and Peter Jennings' ABC program "Common Miracles: The New American Revolution in Learning" (1993) for a window to other extraordinary, paradigm-shattering examples. (See Appendix C.)

INSTRUCTION NEEDS TO CONNECT

The second premise is that effective instruction needs to connect classroom subject matter to students' personal lives — no matter how different those lives may be from the ideal. This connection increases in importance as the California reform effort continues to promote a rich core program of complex knowledge for all children. Again, many educators may comfortably agree with this concept but will have great difficulty in implementing it with consistency or to the extent needed to make schooling effective for most underachieving students. The concept may not be effective in incorporating cultures, values, role models, and points of view into the curriculum, especially for students from diverse backgrounds. True, today's textbooks do a better job of reflecting multicultural concepts than those in the past did and are continuing to improve. The next step, however, will be to help students as individuals better connect what they are learning to their personal lives hour by hour and on a variety of levels: cultural, economic, academic, personal, emotional, and social.

MANY LACK COGNITIVE SECRETS

The third premise is that many underachieving students come to school without the metacognitive repertoire for learning how to learn necessary for academic success. The metacognitive assumptions, strategies, dispositions, and concepts necessary for school success have been referred to as "cognitive secrets." They are used daily, often unconsciously or intuitively, by the most successful learners. Once taught these critical secrets for how to learn, students at risk begin to succeed academically as well. Witness the results at the elementary level with Reading Recovery and at the secondary level with the AVID program as well as the state Tanner projects.

OPPORTUNITY IS NOT ENOUGH

The fourth premise, a critical one, is that access is no longer considered sufficient for all students to enjoy an equal opportunity to learn the district's core curriculum. The philosophy of ESS is that to offer, expose, or provide opportunities is not enough. Students are to be helped to participate in their own construction of knowledge — whether it is original or is found in a rich core curriculum. In addition, student outcomes, behaviors, products, and demonstrated competencies are to reflect significant learning. If students do not show evidence of learning, achieving equal educational opportunity is a hollow pursuit. Both standards — genuine participatory access to a rich curriculum of complex knowledge as well as successful outcomes — must be met to satisfy the goals of ESS.

James Logan High School student, New Haven Unified School District, smiles proudly at graduation.

PREVENTION IS TO REPLACE REMEDIATION

The fifth premise is that prevention should all but replace the traditional concept of remediation. Two levels of prevention are proposed in this initiative. Primary prevention involves providing all students with a rich core curriculum and effective instruction to learn that curriculum. A successful and engaging academic experience for every student will go a long way toward preventing many potential academic, psychological, and social problems. Early childhood education and prenatal care for pregnant teenagers are other strategies that constitute primary prevention. Secondary prevention is intended for students who show signs of incipient problems or are grappling with chronic problems. The goal is to prevent further difficulties while working backwards to deal with the causes of the problems.

Access is no longer considered sufficient for all students to enjoy an equal opportunity to learn the district's core curriculum. Students are to be helped to participate in their own construction of knowledge.

Remediation should focus and build on students' strengths rather than compensate for deficits. Proficiency is developed not by compensating for lack of ability but by extending related knowledge, skills, and experiences that the student already brings to the learning situation. In addition, remediation is most effective if provided as early and as intensively as possible and is short-lived.

Almeria Middle School students from Fontana Unified School District demonstrate their display.

TESTING IS TO BE REPLACED

The sixth premise is that norm-referenced tests should be replaced by portfolio or performance-based assessments (or both) for all students, including students at risk. Because the ESS goals are designed to ensure that as many students as possible learn as much as possible of the core curriculum, assessments need to provide teachers with the information they need to shape their ongoing work with each student. This means that assessments need to provide information on how much of a curriculum each student needs to have mastered. Norm-referenced tests, on the other hand, do not provide direct evidence of how much of a domain students have learned — only how they have performed on the test in comparison with other students in a norming population. The principal goal of assessment in the ESS initiative is not to rank and sort students but to see how much they have learned.

LABELING CAN BE HARMFUL OR HELPFUL

The seventh premise is that identification for enrollment in categorical programs should not produce labels detrimental to a student's success in school. There are two sides to the issue of labeling that present a dilemma for educators everywhere. On the negative side, labels such as *at risk, underachiever, compensatory education student, minority, handicapped,* or *limited-English proficient* can support a self-fulfilling prophecy of failure. Deficits may be implied so that teachers have difficulty in seeing students as individuals with potential for success in school. Such labels support the blame-the-victim syndrome.

On the positive side, labels are often the only vehicle by which students can be identified for needed services and then monitored to assess equal educational opportunity and outcomes. To fail to identify students with whom the school is not successful can result in an out-of-sight, out-of-mind syndrome. For example, until the advent of the *Lau v. Nichols* case in 1975 and subsequent requirements for the state language census, many school districts with hundreds of limited-English-proficient students were reporting fewer than a dozen such students and were ignoring the large number of students who needed special assistance in English and in their home language.

A student from Carver Elementary School in the San Diego City Unified School District shows off his bike-riding skills.

No obvious solution exists as to the problems caused by the identification and labeling of students. However, Marie Clay (1979), author of the Reading Recovery Program, may be near to a solution. Her program works with first graders who are labeled as having reading difficulties. Students are provided with one-to-one tutoring by a highly trained teacher for half an hour a day for approximately 16 weeks in an effort to bring students back into the mainstream of their classrooms. A study comparing the effects of Reading Recovery on a group of students labeled *learning disabled* versus a group labeled *educationally disadvantaged* showed that 70 percent of each group successfully discontinued the program after 12 weeks. Returning to their classrooms, the students were able to perform at the average level of their classmates (Lyons, 1990). Whether they were poor readers because of being disabled or because of being disadvantaged was moot.

Because the same strategy worked equally well for both groups, the original labels eventually seemed pointless. Identifying a student as having reading difficulties appeared to be much less damaging than the other two labels — labels that appear to impugn students' potential. What seems to be important is that educators (1) strive to treat each individual student as one who, given the right treatment, has the potential for success; and (2) then do whatever is necessary to ensure, in the face of any identified difficulties, that the potential is realized.

Paramount Elementary
School classroom
teachers in K-3 identify
students for the Special
Friends Program who
are having difficulty
adjusting to school
and may show acting
out behavior or
moodiness which is
affecting their learn-
ing. Participating
students work one-on-
one with an adult for
one-half hour per week
for 12-15 weeks in the
Azusa Unified School
District program.
(Far West Laboratory
ESS Case Study, 1994)

PERSONAL CONNECTIONS ARE NEEDED

Another premise is the need for personal connections between adults and students and between students and students. If, for example, every student at risk in California had a significant personal connection with an adult (e.g., administrator, specialist, teacher, classified staff person, college or university student, retired adult, or other volunteer as a caring mentor), fewer students would develop a problem that would go unnoticed long enough to become serious or chronic (Benard, 1993). Interestingly, interviews with dropouts reveal disconnection as a major factor in that almost all report having no favorite teacher or class and few if any friends at school before dropping out (Olsen, 1982). Getting students connected to each other through cooperative learning, collaborative projects, and cross-age tutoring has also been shown to be an effective deterrent to poor attendance and has resulted in dramatic reductions in the number of dropouts.

RESOURCES MUST BE USED WELL

The final premise underlying the entire ESS initiative is that schools and school districts can and should be more effective in using existing resources. This issue is sensitive because a lack of adequate funding has affected many desirable programs and activities. In *Savage Inequalities* (1991) Jonathan Kozol makes a convincing case for remedying the blatant funding inequities in some school districts. A recent federal report (Final Report of the National Assessment of the Chapter 1 Program, 1993) reveals that Chapter 1 schools spend more money per child on average than similar non-Chapter 1 schools and usually achieve worse results. Obviously, gross inequities in funding can make a significant difference in the success rate of children in school. Better facilities, better and more materials and equipment, and better training do have a material and psychological impact on teachers and students alike. However, when rates of expenditure *are relatively close*, even schools that get more money may not perform best. In this context, *how* the money is spent becomes the determining factor. For example, approximately two-thirds of Chapter 1 funds in California go to support instructional aides, but research concerning effective services for underachieving students does not support such an expenditure (*CDE Report on Chapter 1 Students*, 1991-92).

Variation in the amount and effect of resources for schools highlights the need for a two-pronged approach to fiscal issues in schools with students at risk. The first approach is to investigate more effective ways of designing and coordinating existing programs and services to maximize their benefits to students. Doing more with existing resources means coordinating staff and funding to ensure that all resources are directed towards the best result in educational outcomes for the lowest-achieving students. The second approach is for the education community to work toward the short-range solution of obtaining grants and gifts and raising funds while working in the Legislature and in the courts toward long-range solutions for equitable funding in all schools.

NEW ROLES FOR IMPLEMENTATION

New roles will be required to make the kinds of significant changes in the status quo necessary for the dramatic improvement of schooling for students at risk (Cummins, 1986). These new or enhanced roles require the following:

◆ **Classroom teachers** willing and able to make decisions on instruction and to be responsible for the successful performance of each student. This effort requires collaboration with parents, specialists, and others to ensure the success of all students at risk. Thus, teachers must become learners as well as effective coordinators of services for their students. They must above all begin to learn how to build on their students' strengths and potential and not simply perpetuate the students' weaknesses by stressing only their needs.

◆ **Specialists** (This category includes but is not limited to those working with Chapter 1, bilingual, and migrant students; alternative education services; special education; gifted and talented education; early primary education; English-language arts, mathematics, and other curriculum areas; and independent study and work experience.) They must be willing and able as partners to collaborate and communicate with each other, with classroom teachers, with child development program staff, and with parents concerning instructional decision making for students with whom they work in common. As with teachers, specialists begin to move toward an approach that builds on students' strengths and potential.

Azusa Unified School District established the District Restructuring Stakeholders Council (DRSC) to rebuild trust, as well as to meet the S.B. 1274 restructuring proposal requirements. Council membership includes representatives from the two employee organizations, the management group, every school in the district, a board member, and the assistant superintendent.
Assistant Superintendent for Educational Services Nancy Moore explained, "We operate on an 'abundance mentality.'"
The district believed DRSC should expand its mission and serve all the schools, not just the ones participating in ESS. Today, all Azusa schools submit their restructuring proposals to the council as part of the approval process. In addition to obtaining district support from proposals and waivers, the council also serves as a clearinghouse of ideas so that all schools may learn about new ideas being implemented in individual schools.
(ESS Update, March 1994)

◆ **Classified staff**, such as paraprofessionals, secretaries, custodians, bus drivers and others, willing and able to take responsibility for the care and academic success of each student with whom they come into contact and perform as active members of the school resources team in supporting the goals and objectives identified for each student and family.

◆ **Parents and families** willing and able to fulfill their rights and responsibilities as partners with school and other agency staff in the joint planning, goal-setting, and intervention strategies necessary to achieve success for their children. The role of parents as key players in promoting effective schooling for their children is distinct from any other role they may play within the community. Parents and schools together share responsibility for the development of comprehensive, continuing programs of effective parent involvement at all grade levels and across all programs. Parent involvement is identified by the California Department of Education and supported by the State Board of Education as a critical dimension of effective schooling.

◆ **Community members** willing and able to commit energy, time, and resources in support of ensuring successful academic outcomes for children, youths, and families in their communities. School districts and schools will be required to explore opportunities and training for community involvement to be involved as partners in the pursuit of excellence in education.

◆ **Principals** capable of being experts in designing and implementing effective curriculum and instruction, organizing effective staff development, promoting meaningful family and community involvement, and administering a coordinated and cohesive school organization. They need to be willing and able to set up structures involving time, money, staff, and communications networks to encourage coordination, risk taking, experimentation, growth, and the pursuit of a vision of success for each student. Principals also need to be willing to work with local businesses, universities, health and social services, and others in their communities to strengthen the role of the school in the community for the benefit of their students.

- ◆ **District office staff** willing and able to support and facilitate school-site planning, decision making, risk taking, and experimentation with policies, money, staff, time, assistance, and other resources as necessary to meet identified goals and objectives of successful academic outcomes for each and every student. What may be a new key area of support to schools and families is the district's role of forging new partnerships with local universities, public and private childrens' services agencies, business, and industry.

- ◆ **District boards of education** willing to waive district policies or procedures that, as demonstrated by school staff and parents, get in the way of achieving student success at a school or in the district as a whole.

- ◆ **Teachers' union leaders** willing to waive contract provisions that, as demonstrated by school staff and parents, get in the way of achieving student success at a school or in the district as a whole.

- ◆ **The California Department of Education and the State Board of Education** willing and able to look at appeals to remove any bureaucratic obstacles to a school's or district's optimal development and performance; provide leadership in curriculum, instruction, materials adoptions, assessment, exemplary school practices, and legislation; broker its services and leadership to schools in greatest need of help; and inform the educational community of successful practices and programs that might serve as models for all.

Whenever Sanborn Elementary School (or any other school working on restructuring in the Alisal Union Elementary School District) seeks a waiver on a district or state policy, their district liaison brings the request before a special committee, the Collaborative Compact, which intervenes on their behalf. Composed of certified and classified union representatives, a board member, district bilingual education coordinator, special education coordinator, and the superintendent, the Collaborative Compact completes all necessary paperwork for state Education Code waivers. (Far West Laboratory ESS Case Study, 1994)

Ultimately, the creation of effective schools for students at risk will depend on the willingness of all of us to work together.

Ultimately, the creation of effective schools for students at risk will depend on the willingness of *all of us* to work together as we (1) experiment to one degree or another with new roles; (2) research and spread new ideas; (3) implement new practices; and (4) set new cultural norms for "how we do things around here" (Deal & Kennedy, 1982). The culture of the school will have to change radically from the status quo if the program is to become more effective with all of its students and their families.

The Department recognizes that a number of districts are already committed to the goals, elements, and roles of the ESS initiative. Many are well on their way to implementing all of these elements; others are just beginning. Through demonstration schools and school districts, the California education community can learn from its ground-breaking efforts and establish a basis for the future support and the promotion of Every Student Succeeds for all schools in California. ❧

Former Santa Ana Unified Superintendent Rudy Castruita encourages schools to look at how they could do things differently to make a difference in educating youth.

SUCCESS FOR EVERY STUDENT IN LEARNING A RICH CORE CURRICULUM

In the Every Student Succeeds initiative, the first two of the six guiding elements also represent the initiative's major goals. The following describes the first goal, which involves a rich core curriculum for all students. This academic component of ESS includes a discussion of the related areas of (1) curriculum; (2) instruction; (3) materials and technology; and (4) assessment. The second guiding element and major goal, a preventive approach, is discussed in Element 2.

RICH CORE CURRICULUM

Curriculum is the stuff of learning, the content to be worked with in class, the knowledge to be created and skills to be developed by students. It should not be an accumulation, no matter how well organized, of a set of isolated facts and skills. Rather, it should be complex, high-status knowledge and skills organized within broad themes, issues, and authentic activities and knowledge products, the kinds that people engage in outside the classroom.

Having all students learn a rich core curriculum is fundamental to the mission of every school and is the first goal of the ESS initiative. However, it is not enough to offer students a choice or the opportunity to learn such a curriculum. To offer or even expose guarantees nothing, although such activities are certainly important first steps. It is still too common — even where an improved curriculum has been developed in a district or school — that the lowest-achieving students are not offered a chance to engage in learning complex, high-status knowledge. The need to acquire basic skills and concepts — or, for immigrant students, the English language — still blocks some students' opportunities to learn a rich curriculum. Grouping and tracking policies and alternate or modified curricula are often warning signs of this problem. Such prerequisites to a meaningful education are inconsistent with the ESS framework as well as the state's curriculum frameworks. Although still very

It is still too common — even where an improved curriculum has been developed in a district or school — that the lowest-achieving students are not offered a chance to engage in learning complex, high-status knowledge. The need to acquire basic skills and concepts — or, for immigrant students, the English language — still blocks some students' opportunities to learn a rich curriculum.

important, basic skills and concepts are best developed in the context of interacting meaningfully with a rich core curriculum.

STUDENT AS SOURCE

What should be the content of this rich curriculum? There are at least four possible sources. The first is the student. That is, some of the stuff of learning in the classroom should be students' background, experiences, values, tastes, aspirations, fears, interests and curiosities, strategies for finding out, insights, and reactions to learning. Recognizing that students are important contributors to the content of the classroom curriculum ensures that they will be active participants, will be motivated, and will have a stake in their own learning. They will also be connected to what is going on in the classroom and have opportunities to find understanding or meaning in new concepts or skills as to what they already know or can do. Including the student as part of the curriculum is one of the most challenging aspects of schooling for California's teachers today, especially in classrooms with students who have experiential, cultural, intellectual, physical, or emotional characteristics different from those who might be considered mainstream students.

Azusa High School students "design a city" on their computers.

TEACHER AS SOURCE

The second source of the curriculum is the teacher; that is, what the teacher already knows, is currently learning, or finds interesting and valuable. Knowledge and skills do not reside only in textbooks, software, curriculum frameworks, or courses of study. If learning involves creating or re-creating knowledge and skills rather than just transmitting and acquiring facts and skills (Wells, 1986), then everyone in class has something to offer or share in a community of inquiry.

Therefore, when students read and share what they have learned, teachers can do the same. When students write, teachers can also write. When students give their reactions and opinions or express interests and curiosities, teachers can share their own as well. Encouraging both students and teachers to contribute to the content of the curriculum in this way supports the personal and social aspects of learning (Smith, 1988; Slavin, et al., 1985; and Wells & Chang-Wells, 1992). It also provides the basis for an investment of energy by teachers and students normally not possible when they are working exclusively on an abstract, imposed body of knowledge that stands as a daily assignment to be completed or a scope and sequence to be covered.

DAILY LIFE AS SOURCE

The third source of curriculum is daily life as it impinges on students and the classroom. Personal, local, national, and international events often arrive with little warning and cannot be planned for or addressed in texts, course outlines, or lesson plans. Yet they represent emotionally powerful opportunities to learn. Topics charged with interest, emotion, and potential for learning might include the death of a local person, a drive-by shooting, a major illness, or a local crisis; a state or national disaster, assassination, election, accident or environmental disaster, political movement, or fad; or an international military crisis, scientific breakthrough, global problem or issue, economic or political summit, or international incident. The classroom curriculum must be flexible and open enough to be able to integrate such items in a timely and effective way if school is to be as meaningful as possible.

SCHOOL CURRICULUM AS SOURCE

Finally, the fourth source of the curriculum, though not the least important, is what is traditionally considered to be the only curriculum, the school curriculum. It is that which the school district believes is crucial for its students to learn as they are preparing for participation in a democracy, the economy, and a healthy life. This curriculum comprises the knowledge and skills outlined in courses of study; in locally adopted grade-level and subject-area curricula; and in textbooks, tests, and related materials. From the point of view of ESS, the best guides for developing this core of knowledge and skills are the state's curriculum frameworks, handbooks, guides, and standards. They are California's current best statements on curriculum and instruction and are developed and endorsed by educational practitioners and leaders from throughout the state. What must be recognized, however, is that what is outlined in these documents is to be provided in a learner-friendly way to *all* students: the bilingual, the economically disadvantaged, the underachieving, the gifted and talented, the average, and the students receiving special education services.

CURRICULUM FRAMEWORKS

The following is a very brief summary of the California frameworks by curriculum area. Again, the primary goal of ESS is to ensure that every student — no matter what his or her group membership, learning characteristics, or future aspirations — be engaged successfully in learning the curriculum from preschool through grade twelve.

1. **English-Language Arts** — A literature-based program in which listening, speaking, reading, and writing are integrated. Students interact with significant core works of literature and confront important human values and issues. Writing is taught as a process, and students find their own voice as authors and write for authentic purposes and audiences. Skills are developed in context to empower students for a wide variety of educational and personal uses of language.

2. **Mathematics** — A problem-solving program in which memorized rules and procedures are second to students' own discovery and understanding of how mathematics works in daily life and in the abstract. All strands of number, measurement, geometry, patterns and functions, statistics and probability, logic, and algebra are integrated into instruction at all grade levels. Numeracy for effective daily living and for higher learning is the goal.

3. **Science** — A program for students to develop high levels of literacy in science through their own observation, interpretation, discovery, and application of scientific concepts, principles, and procedures to historic and contemporary issues and problems in the life, earth, and physical sciences. The curriculum within and across these sciences is organized under themes based on the big ideas in science. New knowledge is built on the experiences and prescientific conceptions of the world students bring to class.

4. **History-Social Science** — A program that incorporates a chronological approach to history as a story well told. The role of circumstances, personalities, choices, values, and ethics are fundamental to understanding in this subject area, as is the role of geography, economics, and sociopolitical systems. Period literature and primary source documents are integrated as students learn of and understand the past and relate it to their daily lives and to the future.

5. **Visual and Performing Arts** — A four-part curriculum involving the content and techniques of dance, drama/theater, music, and the visual arts. Students' learning in each area is guided by a focus on aesthetic perception, creative expression, historical and cultural heritage, and aesthetic valuing. The goal is for students to become lifelong participants in the arts and understand the indispensable role of the arts in culture and daily living.

6. **Health, Physical Education, and Nutrition** — An integrated program to enhance students' capacities for a healthy physical, intellectual, emotional, and social life. The interdependence of nutrition and activity to lifestyle and overall health is central to the curriculum. The responsibility of the individual in relation to society for ensuring a healthy environment for personal and social development is also stressed.

7. **Foreign Language/English as a Second Language (ESL)** — A program based on a communicative rather than a grammar-based approach to developing functional competence in listening, speaking, reading, and writing. Instruction does not involve using English most of the time to talk about the target language. Instead, instruction is *conducted in* the target language and is centered on genuine communicative situations, needs, and functions. The language used is authentic and appears in its cultural context. Offerings include European and, ideally, Pacific Rim languages. American Indian and classical languages as well as American Sign Language are also taught when appropriate. The ESL curriculum begins with survival skills, leading students successfully into the regular English-language arts program and the other subjects in the core curriculum. It is founded on the same principles as those guiding other second-language instruction.

8. **Career-Vocational Education** — Programs in the subject areas of Agriculture, Business, Consumer Home Economics, Health Careers, Home Economics Related Occupations, and Industrial Technology that assist students in making informed career choices. These programs enable students to acquire the knowledge, skills, and understanding necessary to enter and progress in the career area of their choice. Toward that end, programs which integrate the district's core curriculum and the career-vocational curricula are designed and implemented. Career-vocational offerings promote the knowledge, skills, and competencies needed to work and live in a technically advanced and global society, and range from those that require advanced education to those that lead directly to employment.

COMMONALITIES IN THE SCHOOL CURRICULUM

Important features of this core curriculum that are common to each of these subject areas deserve mention. That is, the curriculum advocated for all students is meaning centered in contrast to skills based or fact based. It involves meaning as it relates to students' personal backgrounds and daily lives. This approach is distinguished from more traditional concepts of the curriculum as a linear, sequential accumulation of facts and skills.

Frank Paul Elementary School students from Alisal Union Elementary School District enjoy art class.

Because of its emphasis on meaning and the relationship of school to the real world, this core curriculum is, in effect, contextualized rather than abstract. By contrast, a decontextualized or "de-meaned" curriculum founded on the direct teaching of facts, rules, skills, or algorithms is frequently not engaging enough and does not provide enough opportunities for many students to become intellectually and emotionally involved enough to interact effectively with complex knowledge. More appropriate for all students, especially for students for whom school is not working well, is an academic curriculum that is meaning centered, is broad yet balanced in scope, and ultimately includes crosscurricular themes.

Such themes make it possible to bring literature, history, geography, science, mathematics, art, and vocations together in the service of exploring intrinsically interesting concepts pertinent to the lives of students now and in their future. Major organizing themes might include communication across the ages, friendship and loyalty, service to the local community, time across cultures, inventions, art as a reflection of the times, and so forth. Such a thematic approach will require that a district's core curriculum in each subject area be well developed and approach a state-of-the-art level before attempts are made at thematic integration. Themes and related activities are most powerful when designed around high-quality subject-matter curricula.

Either kind of curriculum, de-meaned or meaningful, may occur in a supplementary program. No guarantee exists that supplementary services provided in class rather than through instruction in a separate setting will be appropriate and effective. All educational services should provide all students with maximum opportunities for their optimal development in a rich, meaning-centered, and thinking curriculum, including students receiving special education services. This requirement applies whether the educational services are core or supplementary or are provided in a nonfunded school or in a Chapter 1 program improvement or schoolwide project; in a primary language or in English; in a vocational or a core class; at an alternative or neighborhood site; or in a mainstream or special day class.

Why is such a curriculum so important for students who are at risk? Many students come from backgrounds and daily lives significantly different from the school environment. They do not easily identify with what goes on in traditional middle-class programs nor in the materials provided by textbook authors writing for middle America. Further, they do not see the relationship between school and their daily or future lives. The discontinuities — whether cultural, linguistic, or socioeconomic — between students' backgrounds and the conventional world of the school and its packaged curriculum make the comprehension of new material very difficult for many.

This contrast between life and school is crucial because what is new must be understood in relation to what is already known if it is to be learned. If the personal experiences of students are not reflected in some way in the program, students remain shut out from any meaningful connections in class. In addition, often faced with a lack of entry-level skills, students never develop the interest and the emotional involvement necessary to invest a substantial amount of energy in schoolwork. For the gap with students at risk to be closed, it is essential to have a meaning-centered, thinking curriculum to which students can make personal contributions and which is offered in a highly interactive context in which students' backgrounds, daily lives, strengths, curiosities, and aspirations are connected.

NEW DIMENSIONS IN THE SCHOOL CURRICULUM

There are two relatively new dimensions to be considered for addition to the school curriculum previously described. Both stand outside of traditional subject-matter knowledge and skills. The first is *group skills and prosocial attitudes and skills*; the second, *metacognition*. Work in this area would help students be more successful in school as well as later in life. The most common reason for people to be fired from a job in the U.S. is their inability to get along with their fellow workers (Kagan, 1988). Because most lines of work involve teamwork to a greater or lesser degree, it would be helpful if students consciously learned how to work together toward a common goal rather than be given only a steady diet of competitive or individual forms of activity in school (Kohn, 1986).

Special relationships are developed at Carver Elementary School, San Diego City Unified School District.

Formal versions of cooperative learning (Johnson, Johnson, & Holubec, 1986; Cohen, 1986; Kagan, 1988; and Slavin, 1983) represent one family of options for promoting prosocial skills and attitudes. A second is to promote more collaborative projects resulting in a group product (e.g., a poll or survey, a case study or local history, an investigative report on a problem in the local community, a class newspaper, a film, an analysis of the city's water, a play). For such projects the work agenda might include a focus on a few group skills per week, with teacher-led debriefings of not only the work in progress but also of how the team is doing on this week's group skills (e.g., taking turns, contributing ideas, being brief, not dominating, refraining from personal criticisms).

PROSOCIAL SKILLS AND ATTITUDES

The development of *prosocial skills and attitudes* is closely related to cooperation and good group skills. For prosocial growth students might be helped to develop a willingness to accept and give help, a sense of responsibility for their own learning as well as that of their classmates, the ability to see the world from another person's point of view, a willingness to accept differences of opinion and agree to disagree, and the capacity to give as well as accept praise. Again, work on authentic projects in a group setting provides a perfect opportunity for teachers to promote such an agenda. The kind of social and emotional development that can result from a focus on group and prosocial skills can begin to pave the way for many students and teachers to focus on and achieve dramatic gains in academic achievement (Comer, 1988). The most promising long-term project in California is being conducted by Eric Schaps in San Mateo. (See Appendix C.) For over a decade teachers have pioneered ways of promoting prosocial development among students as a daily part of the curriculum (Schaps & Solomon, 1990).

METACOGNITION

The second new dimension to be added to the classroom curriculum is *metacognition.* Here we are referring to the concepts and competencies that make it possible for a student to function optimally in school. They go beyond critical thinking, higher-order thinking, or study skills and are the unwritten, unspoken cognitive secrets that teachers and successful students use, often unconsciously or even intuitively, to make the best of their potential in school. In short, they are the concepts, strategies, assumptions, beliefs, dispositions, and perspectives that involve *learning how to learn* and include such notions as the following:

1. Effort relates directly to outcomes (Dweck, 1983).
2. One has extensive control over the course of one's life, especially in terms of schooling outcomes (internal locus of control).
3. Intelligence is incremental and is not an inherent static capacity (Dweck, 1986).
4. College and the professions are for "people like me."
5. It is legitimate to disagree with what is in print.
6. School is supposed to make sense.
7. "If I try, I can."
8. Confidence and hard work will result in student learning and development (Howard, 1993).

Metacognition also involves *cognitive strategies* that provide a basis for how to learn. They include strategies for finding out what is important or what is expected — an ability especially important for knowing what to pay attention to in class, in a textbook, in researching a report, or on a test. Using mind maps and organizing structures, such as outlines and hierarchies, are effective cognitive strategies. Other strategies include trying to understand theme and variation or the concept of the transferability of an underlying principle to other contexts; asking what-if questions or hypothesizing and guessing; disagreeing with or looking for consistency in material presented; and determining whether the connotative or denotative right answer is the "best" one to mark on a standardized test. Weinstein and Mayer (1986) summarize the field of research on learning strategies by identifying five categories:

1. Rehearsal strategies: repeating information orally or in writing, underlining or highlighting written material
2. Elaboration strategies: forming mental images, paraphrasing, summarizing

3. Organizational strategies: making lists and hierarchies, outlining

4. Comprehension monitoring strategies: questioning self, using questions in a textbook to guide reading

5. Affective and motivational strategies: reducing external distractions, controlling fears of failure, concentrating

Reading Recovery (1979), the one-to-one tutoring intervention for first graders developed by Marie Clay in New Zealand, is only one example of an approach that promotes cognitive and metacognitive strategies and concepts related to reading rather than skills or knowledge in the traditional sense. This intervention is particularly helpful for students who come to school without the benefit of hundreds or thousands of hours of literacy experiences. (The range in the U.S. is zero to 2,000 hours of literacy experiences for kindergartners.) Such experiences provide most children with concepts, assumptions, skills, and knowledge that make them ready to learn to read when they reach school. However, children who do not develop this cognitive and metacognitive repertoire related to reading can become successful readers if given assistance.

In *Reading Recovery* or *Descubriendo la lectura* (the Spanish version), the teacher allows the student to control all the processing in the act of reading. This approach promotes confidence as well as cognitive reading strategies and assumptions that children at risk often lack. Included in this approach are such strategies and assumptions as (1) print is meaningful and imitates speech; (2) there are spaces between words; (3) one can guess at a word; (4) visual cues in a story may be used to understand it; (5) one can self-correct; (6) one can reread stories to get better and to enjoy them more; (7) one can draw on background experiences and personal reactions to read words and understand stories; and (8) one can read on without knowing every word. Contrast these strategies with the only strategies that poor readers report using when they get stuck on a word: (1) "I try to sound it out;" or (2) "I ask the teacher."

When the lowest-achieving first-grade students spend 15 to 20 weeks specifically developing these concepts, assumptions, and strategies that efficient readers already control, 70 percent to 90 percent of them never need reading remediation again. These students have been followed for as many as four years after the intervention and continue to function at levels comparable to or superior to their peers in reading. They now have skills for how to learn and solve problems no matter what new demands are made in the curriculum. *Reading Recovery* can

Alisal Community School is focused on literacy proficiency and has adopted Reading Recovery as a major intervention strategy for its primary-grade students. (CDE Staff Visit, 1994)

serve as an excellent prototype for home-grown interventions that might be developed in any subject area at any grade level.

Besides *Reading Recovery* there are other programs and strategies that directly or indirectly promote learning-how-to-learn strategies, concepts, and assumptions.

In *Reciprocal Teaching* (Palincsar & Brown, 1984), for example, the teacher models four reading-comprehension strategies with a small group of students. The strategies include summarizing, questioning, clarifying, and predicting. Eventually, the teacher gives each student a turn to be "in the driver's seat" and to direct classmates in the use of the four strategies during small-group reading lessons. This activity is intended for students who already decode. The results show the lowest readers achieving levels of comprehension of the best readers. Good readers improve significantly as well; but with the poorest readers achieving the most, this strategy counts as a gap closer.

In *Directed Reading Thinking Activities* (DRTA) (Stauffer, 1970), another strategy for building comprehension strategies, the teacher begins by helping students connect an upcoming lesson, film, or reading with their personal backgrounds. Students learn to generate hypotheses or questions about what they may encounter in the material to be presented or read. They go through the material independently and discuss the evidence for their various hypotheses or answers to their questions, learning to cite specific passages to support their points of view. This kind of preview activity that focuses on meanings has proven more powerful at increasing comprehension than other helpful but less effective approaches that preview difficult vocabulary items or grammatical structures (Krashen, 1988).

Finding Out/Descubrimiento (FO/D) (DeAvila & Duncan, 1982) for science and mathematics is a collection of hands-on experiments and data-collection projects in Spanish and English. Besides learning the subject matter, students acquire useful learning strategies, such as how to collaborate with peers, organize information, pay attention to critical details, develop and defend hypotheses, and conduct measurements by means of conventional and unconventional metrics.

Available for the development of higher-order critical-thinking skills are such programs as Project IMPACT; Higher Order Thinking Skills (HOTS); Instrumental Enrichment; Creative Problem Solving; the Cognitive Research Trust (CoRT) Program (de Bono, 1989); and Guilford's Structure of the

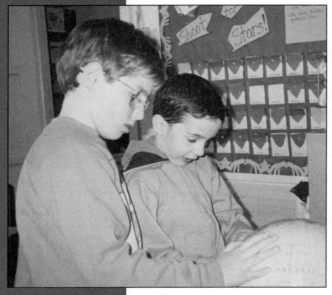

Students travel "around the world" at West Randall Elementary School, Fontana Unified School District.

Intellect (SOI). With these programs teachers can help students work with the curriculum more critically and effectively.

The various thinking mathematics curricula now available commercially, as well as the Department of Education's Math A and Math B, also help students develop more than basic mathematical concepts, facts, and operations. The students are assisted in improving their options on how to approach mathematics and how to solve problems — in short, how to learn.

Finally, Jeff Howard's Efficacy Program shows great promise of influencing children's theories of intelligence and their notions of what it takes to be a successful learner. Basing the program in large part on Carol Dweck's research on children's concepts of intelligence, Howard has come up with a formula for helping to promote the developmental rather than the static theory of intelligence. This contrast is very similar to the major difference in cultural viewpoints reported between the U.S. and Japanese cultures (Fallows, 1989; Stevenson & Stigler, 1992). Whereas talent and intelligence are considered major factors in a person's success here, hard work is seen as the predominant explanatory factor for success in Japan. Howard works with schools to help them teach students the formula *Think You Can + Work Hard = Get Smart.* Some students may be naturally more well endowed than others in some ways, but effort seems to be a better guarantee of success than innate talent. Dweck (1986) has found that children who believe in the latter theory are particularly at risk of an academic crisis as they confront an often precipitous increase in cognitive demand in the curriculum when they transfer from elementary school to junior high school, middle school, or high school.

Exploration of this new domain of cognitive secrets should be particularly profitable for students at risk of failure and for students having problems with subject matter at any grade level. Armed with the proper cognitive and metacognitive assumptions, concepts, and strategies, virtually all students have the capacity to function successfully and learn to cope with whatever curriculum demands they are likely to face.

INSTRUCTION

Instruction designed to promote a community of inquiry in the classroom or at alternative sites in the community allows students to interact intensely with each other, the teacher, and the curriculum. In such a community everyone is a teacher, and everyone is a learner. With 30 students and one teacher in class, there are 31 learners and, perhaps more importantly, 31 teachers.

INTERACTION

In programs organized according to this metaphor of a "community of inquiry," as many or more questions come from students as from teachers. Students are encouraged to ask and answer questions and are given time to do so. In addition, students talk more than the teacher does. Schoolwork is made understandable in terms of students' experiences, values, tastes, and aspirations. Students spend a significant part of the day in study groups or interest groups organized around themes that exclude no one because of differential skills. Teachers become learners, too, and share their discoveries and products with their students as they have their students share with them. They also play the role of mentor or master craftsperson in certain learning domains while students participate as cognitive apprentices (Resnick & Klopfer, 1989). In all cases, teachers maintain a fundamental posture of advocacy for each student's strengths and potential rather than reinforce the perception of student "needs" in terms of academic deficits.

Classroom activity needs to be highly interactive, with students interacting intensively in four domains:

◆ Student with teacher: discussion, questions and answers, mutual feedback

◆ Student 1 with student 2: exchanges within dyad, cooperative, or collaborative learning activities

◆ Student with text: responses to written, aural, visual, or kinesthetic text

◆ Student 1 with student 1: personal reflections, writings in a learning log, and so on

The interactions in this typology are most powerful when they are *two-way* (Long, 1985); that is, when both parties have information or a service to provide that the other needs, (e.g., a jigsaw cooperative learning activity in which each student on the team becomes an expert in some part of the final task). If they cannot be interdependent in this way, interactions can at least be *reciprocal one-way* exchanges, (e.g., "First you quiz me; then I'll quiz you"). When teachers ask questions of a student only to get right answers, the interaction is one-way. When teachers ask questions to learn about a student's experiences, point of view, or reaction to a given lesson, there is no single right answer but only information that the student alone can provide. The result is more of a two-way exchange between *informational equals* (Wells, 1986). Such an interaction inevitably leads to an exchange between the student and teacher that is more two-way and more powerful in promoting learning than traditional one-way exchanges.

Research on highly interactive approaches, such as cooperative learning in social studies (Cohen, 1986; Slavin, 1983), hands-on science learning coupled with performance-based testing (Steinberg, 1990), and reciprocal teaching in reading (Palincsar, 1984), for example, support this statement. Although high, middle, and low achievers do better than control groups on these activities, the lowest achievers consistently make the largest gains. These strategies help them to accelerate. They are, in short, *gap-closing strategies*. A crucial point should be made here about the powerful interactive strategy of cooperative learning. Whether the teacher employs a cooperative learning strategy developed by Slavin (1983), the Johnsons (1986), Cohen (1986), or Kagan (1988), research studies indicate that significant academic results are achieved only when two essential features are present; that is, when *both individual and group rewards* are made an integral part of the strategy.

TEACHER- AND STUDENT-CENTERED LEARNING OPPORTUNITIES

A balance of *teacher- and student-centered learning* is also an important consideration where students have not only *responsibility* for but also *control* over:

- ◆ What they learn
- ◆ How they learn it
- ◆ When they know it — at least some of the time

Student-centered activity may include very structured cooperative learning as well as more informal collaborative learning activities. Examples of student-centered activities include group projects, cross-age tutoring, reciprocal teaching, children reading to each other and to their parents at home, interactive journals, development of a classroom library of student-made books, student-made test questions, and student-conducted surveys and polls.

Students also need to learn to function successfully in a variety of *grouping configurations* if they are to be prepared to meet the demands of lifelong learning and work. Included might be homogeneous and heterogeneous groupings as well as individual, paired, small-group, and whole-class learning options.

A culture of failure develops when students of the same age and grade level are consistently grouped in designated low-achieving groups, in the regular classroom, in pull-outs, or even in special day classes. That is, students begin to see themselves as failures. Students in these situations often reinforce a norm of low achievement even in the face of student successes: "You're just showing off." "You must have cheated." "You're just as dumb as the rest of us." (Featherstone, 1987)

When it is appropriate to group students by skill level, the potential negative effects of grouping can be mitigated by making the groupings temporary. For some activities groups could be organized which consist of some students performing at their normal grade level, younger students working above their grade level, and older students working below. This kind of grouping is known as the Joplin Plan and is used by Robert Slavin in his Success for All Program in Baltimore (Slavin, 1994).

All grouping should have clear educational purposes, last a relatively short time, not result in dead-end tracking, and not disadvantage students in their optimal academic, psychological, or social development. Frequent reorganizing of groups of slow, average, and fast students (at least every eight weeks) at different grade levels in reading or mathematics, for example, will likely prevent students from developing a low academic self-concept as a result of group membership.

Instruction conducted as described above suggests that a focus on important *skills and facts through direct teaching* and seat work would no longer consume most of the day. Instead, many of these skills and much of this academic knowledge could be:

◆ Acquired as a by-product of authentic activity
◆ Taught at teachable moments
◆ Worked on during mini lessons or brief asides in the meaningful context of an authentic activity

The most effective classroom activity should engage students cognitively, behaviorally, and emotionally. The better the program in all three domains, the better will be the chances for students at risk to experience a turnaround in their school performance.

Educators need to be aware, however, that there are *good, better, and best strategies* and that perhaps good strategies should be jettisoned to make way for better or best ones. For example, in a meta-analysis of instructional strategies reported by Bloom (1984), some strategies, such as using advanced organizers, have been found to produce an average gain of .20 standard deviations. On the other hand, peer and cross-age tutoring resulted in an average .40 standard deviation gain — twice as much. Cooperative learning produced an average .80 standard deviations gain, which is four times the progress achieved with advanced organizers; and one-to-one tutoring produced a 2.00 gain, which is ten times the power of using advanced organizers! And virtually any of these strategies, if applied appropriately, could overcome the negative effect of low socioeconomic status calculated at a .25 standard deviation. For the sake of underachievers who need a means to accelerate their learning, the significance of exploring and incorporating only the most powerful strategies in the classroom becomes obvious if not critical.

Effectiveness of Instructional Strategies
(Bloom,1984)

Strategy	Average gain in standard deviations
Advanced Organizers	.20
Peer and Cross-age Tutoring	.40
Cooperative Learning	.80
One-to-one Tutoring	2.00

An excellent source of learning about a wide variety of instructional strategies refined by educators over the years can be found in the "Four Families of Teaching Strategies," outlined in *Models of Teaching* (Joyce & Weil, 1980). More than 80 instructional strategies have been identified and are categorized under these families, named for the general student outcomes that are characteristic of the strategies. The families are (1) behavioral; (2) information processing (including critical thinking); (3) social interaction (including cooperative learning); and (4) personal. Teachers who have been trained, for example, in several teaching strategies, such as concept attainment, Socratic questioning, inquiry learning, synectics, and lesson design possess a valuable repertoire that should be drawn upon to plan lessons conducted and organized in a variety of ways to capture the interests and energies of a variety of students. Finally, another rich source of strategy research is the American Educational Research Association's *Handbook of Research on Teaching* (1986). This volume contains a summary of research in effective instructional strategies, in a variety of subject areas, for different ethnic groups and participants in categorical programs as related to metacognition. This work is not to be overlooked in the search of better or best strategies for underachieving students.

Activities conducted in students' preferred *learning styles, modes, and languages* are another critical dimension of promoting all students' intense participation and high investment of effort in class. Learning opportunities should be provided in the student's strongest language, which for many immigrant students is their home language. This is the best response to the question, "How can you teach students what they don't know in a language they can't understand?" And research (Ramirez, 1991; and Willig, 1985) clearly supports the efficacy of sound bilingual approaches that promote *additive, proficient bilingualism* over English-only approaches. Lambert and Peale (1962), Cummins (1981), and Duncan and DeAvila (1982) have all reviewed research on the cognitive advantages that additive proficient bilingualism has over even the highest-performing monolinguals of

Students at Almeria Middle School, Fontana Unified School District, learn about Egypt through art.

either language. These advantages range from higher IQ scores to improved divergent thinking to an overall increased cognitive flexibility, especially in word usage and problem solving. Hearing of such findings, parents of monolingual English speakers force school districts to offer their children Canadian-style immersion programs or, better, two-way bilingual programs in which majority and minority speakers are immersed in the minority language beginning in kindergarten to develop additive proficient bilingualism, biliteracy, and biculturalism.

Although most effective in the context of a well-designed bilingual program, *sheltered English instruction* does produce better results than the old-fashioned sink-or-swim approach or submersion endured by immigrants in the early part of the century. It is most appropriate for intermediate speakers of English and becomes a last resort for educators with students for whom bilingual teachers, aides, and materials in the home language are not available. Further, it is designed to make instruction in the district's core curriculum comprehensible for non-native speakers. Sheltered English instruction (1) is meaning-based rather than grammar-based; (2) makes extensive use of contextual clues, such as props, situations, and, most importantly, students' own background knowledge; and (3) includes healthy doses of interdependent student interactions, such as those found in cooperative learning and authentic collaborative projects.

Students at Frank Paul Elementary School, Alisal Union Elementary School District, spend time in the Primary Academic Lab.

However, to prevent the development of *limited, subtractive bilingualism* through loss of a minority-status home language as English is acquired, the school should promote the development of the child's mother tongue at home and in the community if it cannot be done at school. Studies conducted among inner-city Chinese LEP students have found that community-based multiple sites of learning exist in major cities (Chang, 1993; Chang & Fung, 1994). Home language development and biliteracy are possible when the child finds mother-tongue support in at least two out of three contexts of home, school, and community.

Students who are native speakers of English may use a dialect, such as *Black English* (also referred to as Black Language, Ebonics, or Nonstandard English). In this case it is important to begin instruction with what the student brings to class, the student's home dialect. The teacher should validate the student's speech, help him or her acquire a more standard school dialect, and clarify the contexts and purposes for the effective use of one or the other form of speech. As with students who come to school with a home language other than English, the goal is to promote additive rather than subtractive language acquisition. A second language or dialect is acquired in *addition* to what the student already brings to school, not as a *replacement* of his/her home language or dialect. The State-Sponsored Standard English Proficiency Program, directed through the Department of Education's Compensatory Education Office, is a good source of information on this strategy. (See Appendix C.)

As to *learning styles and modes*, the teacher should identify and capitalize on students' preferred approaches first. These might range from independent to group activities, structured lessons to open-ended projects, abstract to hands-on lessons, and gestalt to linear/sequential organizations of material. Other approaches range from "show me" (field-sensitive) to "tell me" to "let me figure it out on my own" (field-independent), not to mention modal preferences, such as visual, auditory, kinesthetic, and eclectic. Capitalizing on *preferred* styles or modes is

At Sanborn Elementary School, where only 13 percent of the students are native English speakers, students are first sorted by language development stage (Spanish, transitional, post-transitional, English only) and grade level. Classes are grouped heterogeneously by gender, behavior, and academic ability, and resource specialist students are integrated throughout.
(Far West Laboratory ESS Case Study, 1994)

insufficient in itself to enhance the students' success, however. The next step in promoting students' capacities to function effectively *in their nonpreferred modes and styles* must also be included on the teacher's agenda so that students will have the versatility they need to succeed in a variety of learning contexts in school and in life.

In a related area to learning styles, Howard Gardner (1983, 1993) has enriched the notion of intelligence by outlining *seven intelligences* that students can draw on and that should be further developed in school. Expanding schooling to incorporate and value all seven would give more students a better chance to be successful academically and, in general, to experience optimal development of all of their potential. The seven include:

1. Linguistic
2. Logical-mathematical
3. Spatial
4. Kinesthetic
5. Musical
6. Interpersonal
7. Intrapersonal intelligences

Unfortunately, many schools place the highest value on the first two items and spend most of their time developing and evaluating only those two. Even in the linguistic domain, reading and writing are often valued to the virtual exclusion of aural and oral development. A classroom that promotes and values work done in all seven of the intelligences in each major unit of study would go a long way to opening school to the possibility of success for each student.

Regardless of learning style, mode, or intelligence, however, learning activities are more likely to be effective if *authentic*. This instructional concept is aligned with that of a curriculum that is meaning-centered and contextualized rather than skill-centered and abstract. Authentic activities include projects, jobs, or services patterned after what adults do. Thus, students might be involved in a Foxfire-type local history project, ethnography, or investigative report regarding a local community problem; political letter writing; public speaking for persuasive, informative, or entertainment purposes; dramatic, comic, or musical performances of various kinds; Model United Nations and other simulations; student newspapers and book publishing; artistic and musical projects; the development, administration, and analysis of polls and surveys; fund-raising or business-oriented activities; political cartooning; and so forth.

In a related area to learning styles, Howard Gardner (1983, 1993) has enriched the notion of intelligence by outlining seven intelligences that students can draw on and that should be further developed in school.

Students at Carver Elementary School, San Diego Unified School District, prepare for driving.

Consider the following example for *English as a Second Language* (ESL) students. Immigrant parents, often unfamiliar with local markets, do not know where to find bargains when shopping for food. There is usually a range of prices for a typical shopping basket of goods among several stores in most urban and suburban areas. Sometimes, local news stations even provide weekly comparisons for their viewers. As a powerful learning activity as well as a help to their parents, ESL students could do their own authentic shopping-basket survey of local markets by combing through weekly advertisements, visiting the markets to survey prices, or both. The authentic product would be a written and oral report to parents on a comparison of prices that might include a student-developed survey and charts and bar graphs illustrating the pricing study. For the students such a project would be an effective orientation to local culture, a rich source of vocabulary development, and an effective exercise in realistic arithmetic and statistics. The parents would undoubtedly be helped to stretch their food dollars, which for some would be as good as getting a raise in pay.

To capitalize on authentic classroom activities and projects, the school might put on a student-developed and student-presented conference at the end of the semester or year. Students would be helped to organize it and make presentations. There might be keynote addresses, workshops, mini-institutes and seminars, panels, entertainment, artwork, brochures, posters, handouts, publications, exhibits, registration, name tags, luncheons with speakers — everything one might see at a professional conference. Students would have an audience of their peers, their parents, and community members to appreciate and to learn from the authentic projects completed during the year.

Also, students could participate in service learning whereby their community service experience is based on a legitimate community need (e.g., restoring a dead stream; providing assistance to elderly persons in nursing homes, tutoring younger, less successful students) and is linked to their core curriculum. Such teaching and learning are powerful instructionally and teach personal and social responsibility, self-esteem, and citizenship (Conrad & Hedin, 1989).

Authentic learning activities and projects often have to take place — at least to some degree — outside the traditional classroom or even the school site. Such activities clearly redefine if not completely outdate the traditional concept of *homework*. Students find themselves learning outside the classroom not because an assignment has been made merely to be handed in and corrected but because they are intrinsically motivated to complete a project that incorporates their own vested interests. Older students might even enroll in alternative educational programs, sometimes conducted at a different school site or at nonschool sites that take advantage of the community as classroom.

MATERIALS AND TECHNOLOGY

Materials and equipment serve a supportive rather than a central role in the curriculum and instruction outlined previously. That is, the school districts' core curricula and the teachers' instructional strategies should not be dictated by textbooks. Because the curriculum comes from four sources — the child, the teacher, life, and the district's adopted core curriculum and textbooks — commercial materials should support rather than mandate instruction. Effective schooling thus becomes much more than the acting out of scripts written by the publishers of textbooks and tests. On the other hand, materials and equipment aligned with and used in the curriculum and instruction described previously can be indispensable for each student's academic success.

Because the curriculum and instruction presented here are much broader, more authentic, interactive, and meaning-centered than traditional approaches to schooling, teachers will need time to work with each other and assistance in gathering more authentic, primary source materials; doing research and developing authentic activities, units, and themes; and planning together as they divide the labor of such a monumental undertaking. Dumping boxes of new materials on isolated teachers will simply be counterproductive in such a reform effort.

Some key characteristics of effective instructional materials are the following:

1. Strong correlation with the state curriculum frameworks, guides, handbooks, and standards
2. Accurate and authentic content
3. Deep and broad content
4. Lively, engaging narrative

5. Richness in visual and format features that clarify, enrich, and extend the content

6. Cultural diversity in content and in the language(s) and dialects used for the text (e.g., English, primary languages other than English, sheltered English, and examples of nonstandard dialects when appropriate)

7. Comprehensiveness and diversity, including primary source materials, tradebooks, fiction and nonfiction, supplementary resources, and multimodal features (e.g., printed text, visuals, video and/or compact discs, audio, and hands-on materials)

8. Supportive technology, including computers, video equipment, cameras, recorders, calculators, and other electronic equipment as well as graphic materials, models, manipulatives, and realia

9. Assessments that are performance-based or include guidelines for portfolios tied to a rubric of standards and aligned with the curriculum and instruction that students have experienced

Students at West Randall Elementary School, Fontana Unified School District, learn their way "around the nation."

Unfortunately, even the newest electronic devices may not help improve students' access to and success in the district's curriculum. Technology may be employed in the service of a traditional, decontextualized, skills-based, teacher-centered curriculum and instructional program or may support the opposite. The ESS initiative supports the use of technology for the latter.

The ESS framework promotes the use of technology in the service of a combined teacher-centered and student-centered program. Students should be able to control what they do or produce with whatever equipment may be available. For example, they might use technology to create, discover, make a presentation with a variety of media, or communicate with people in different contexts or over long distances. Using video equipment to create a program for a local cable channel or send to a sister class in another community, state, or country is a more effective use of technology than having a teacher simply record the school's Christmas or Cinco de Mayo programs to store on a shelf.

Four basic uses of a computer in school are:

1. **Finding information** — using the computer as an electronic encyclopedia, dictionary, or thesaurus or using a program such as Compuserve or Prodigy

2. **Creating information** — using the computer for word processing, desktop publishing, creating computer graphics, creating animation, or programming

3. **Practicing skills or playing games** — using the computer in an interactive and often repetitive manner for enjoyment or reinforcement

4. **Interacting with other people** — exchanging information through telecommunications, modems, faxes, newsletters, bulletin boards, pen pal programs in the U.S. and abroad, and so forth

Basic uses of a computer
1. Finding information
2. Creating information
3. Practicing skills or playing games
4. Interacting with other people

Using a computer for creating a class newsletter, designing student greeting cards, writing letters to the newspaper or legislature, telecommunicating with students in other communities or countries (especially in languages other than English), publishing student writings for the school library, writing a computer program, or creating original computer graphics, musical arrangements, or animations will undoubtedly have a greater impact on student achievement than more skills- or game-oriented programs.

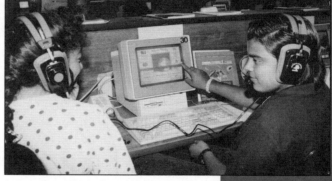

Cooperative groups study geography through interactive multimedia programs at Lathrop Intermediate School, Santa Ana Unified School District.

Used properly, technology will facilitate students' intense, two-way interactions with the school's curriculum, their own personal curriculum, and the curriculum of daily life around them. It will engage them and motivate them while allowing them to develop a command of the media and instruments that are becoming fundamental in our changing society. Technology in the service of drill and practice or fun and games becomes little more than an electronic pencil, work sheet, or game board, with the impact as negligible as the cost is prohibitive. Of course, schools must strive to be technologically up-to-date. But money cannot be invested lightly on technological appearances at the expense of more effective ways of helping every student achieve academic success, with or without technology. The ultimate issue is *what* students are learning and *how well and how fast* are they learning it. If technology helps, fine. But if there are other ways to accomplish the task without technology, then students should be provided with whatever it takes to succeed.

ASSESSMENT OF STUDENT LEARNING

Ideally, assessment of student performance should be conducted in the *same mode as instruction*. Although some evidence exists that students educated in holistic, interactive, meaning-centered ways can outperform, even on skills-based tests, students taught facts and skills in the traditional way (*Teaching Advanced Skills to Educationally Disadvantaged Students*, March, 1991), the curriculum, instruction, and assessment should be aligned.

AUTHENTIC PERFORMANCE-BASED ASSESSMENTS

Eventually, the traditional system of discrete-point (multiple choice), norm-referenced tests designed to rank-order students by percentile according to their recall or recognitions of isolated facts and skills will have to be abandoned. It will be replaced by a more direct measure of a student's mastery in a given domain of knowledge; that is, by authentic, performance-based assessments. The California Learning Assessment System (CLAS) provides such an assessment for language arts, science, and history-social science. It goes well beyond the bubble to provide an authentic, indeed, an integrated assessment device to examine student performance in grades four, eight, ten, and twelve.

A word of caution is in order, however. Even a well-designed performance-based test can be as misused, in some respects, as a norm-referenced, discrete-point test, especially if it is given only once a year. To draw inferences or conclusions with confidence about what a child may have learned throughout the year or to attempt to predict future student performance from a single-incident test is unreliable.

A better system is to triangulate a judgment of a student's learning. That is, multiple measures are used, such as the results of multiple performance-based assessments collected throughout the year, portfolios of student work, student-teacher-parent feedback surveys, and the traditional end-of-the-year test, such as CLAS. At the level of the classroom unit or thematic project, triangulation may mean collecting data on the *quantity*, *quality*, and *level of difficulty* of student work, with a four- to six-point rubric or scale assigned to each area. A student's performance could be triangulated by synthesizing the teacher's rating, rating of the student's peers, and the student's self-rating.

ANALYZING DATA

The data collected from any of these sources or at any level should be subject to district- or school-developed benchmarks of grade-level or competence level outlined in a rubric. The California Learning Record is a good example of a qualitative information-collecting protocol for classroom teachers, at least as to literacy development. It includes a rubric outlining levels of development beginning in kindergarten and establishing a benchmark of competence by grade two. A version of this instrument for grades three through twelve has also been developed.

Although it is advocated that assessments be used for measuring absolute levels of performance or mastery of knowledge in a given domain — as opposed to simply rank-ordering students by means of percentiles — there is still a need to consider two other features in an assessment system. The first is to look at student performance in terms of *absolute levels of achievement or mastery in a given domain.* It is not as important for ESS purposes to know whether a student did better or worse than another on an assessment. It is more important to know how much mathematics, science, social science, language arts, and so on, a child has learned. What capacities has the student developed to orchestrate facts, ideas, conceptual frameworks, assumptions, strategies, dispositions, and skills to solve problems or create knowledge products? To what degree has the school been successful with each student relative to desired academic outcomes, psychological outcomes, and social outcomes? Given that the school community will not be successful at helping each student reach benchmarks of success by a given grade level, there needs to be another way of looking at outcome data besides that of determining how many students have succeeded or failed.

A second way is to look at *gains or progress* toward mastery relative to district benchmarks as discussed above. Since many students are not achieving at desired levels of competence according to district or school targets, the adults at a school need to know how they are doing with each student in order to have a fighting chance of intervening effectively and in a timely way for each child's success. If a student is not performing at a given grade-level benchmark and is not making significant gains toward that standard, the school needs to mobilize its resources immediately to accelerate that child's progress.

In either case the data should be analyzed *by student* for reasons just mentioned. It should also be available *by student population.* Comparisons of outcomes by student population are crucial for determining *equity of outcomes*, especially as to gender, ethnicity, socioeconomic level, categorical program participation, and English language proficiency.

Some seventh-grade students at Fern Bacon Middle School organized their work portfolios, making presentations to invited educators, local businessmen/women, and adults from the community on Portfolio Day. (CDE Staff Visit, 1994)

Comparisons of outcomes by student population are crucial for determining equity of outcomes, especially as to gender, ethnicity, socioeconomic level, categorical program participation, and English language proficiency.

Much more controversial would be the equity of outcomes analyzed by school or even by classroom. Because a constellation of circumstances is usually responsible for low outcomes, such a review would have to be done *not for criticizing* but for providing the intense assistance that staff and students need to ensure that student performance is raised quickly to acceptable levels.

Collecting, displaying, and analyzing data by such categories at various grade levels and in different subject areas can be a daunting task for a school or district to set up. It takes a substantial investment of time, ingenuity, and money but is the only way a school or district can ensure the outcome feedback necessary to improve itself at helping each child become successful. Such an analysis is also now required as part of the state Coordinated Compliance Review under Integrated Programs Item 3.

Other data are useful to a school or school district beyond academic performance outcomes. It does little good to praise ourselves too much for great reports on students' academic performance when dropout rates are very high. The school community must look at secondary data, such as the *School Performance Report*; information on referrals by student population; dropout rates; numbers of library books checked out; attendance; award recipients; and the results of academic contests, fairs, or tournaments, especially if displayed and analyzed by students. In addition, schools may want to consider surveys of the attitudes of parents, staff, and students; classroom observations to determine the degree of implementation of new practices; an analysis of student work and comparisons of the school's program with the key ideas in the state program quality criteria; information on levels of parent and community participation; and any other qualitative or quantitative data that might be considered useful as important indicators of a school's performance with its students at risk.

USES OF ASSESSMENT DATA

How might assessment data be used? First, classroom teachers should have assessment feedback on student performance as often as possible if they are to be successful with each student by name and intervene in a timely way when necessary. Portfolios have been a blessing for teachers fortunate enough to have such a system in place. But data collected at the school level need to be fed back to teachers and analyzed by the school community as well so that appropriate changes or interventions might be initiated for the benefit of each student or student population.

A *flagging system* should be developed at the classroom and school levels to identify students or student populations having difficulties. Portfolios, use of periodic running records of students' reading performance, collection of data on the *California Learning Record*, a quarterly review of grades or other more enlightened performance indicators, and Student Study Teams are a few of the possible features of a school's flagging system that will help prevent a child's being left behind.

Besides being used to inform teachers' interventions, assessment information should be used to *reveal student strengths and potential*, not just weaknesses. This idea of building on student strengths, especially by using formal assessment data, has not been well developed. Outcomes, especially those of low-performing students, have long attracted those performing assessments. They prefer to see the cup half empty rather than half full. Cummins (1986) admonishes us to shift from an assessment system that disables children by legitimizing their weaknesses to one that advocates for their strengths and potential. And it all comes down to seeing the same data through different filters and for different purposes.

Marie Clay's *Observation Survey* (1993), a diagnostic test of first graders having trouble with reading, is a classic example of using data to build on strengths. During the assessment students are asked, among other things, to identify as many letters of the alphabet, to read as many words from a list as possible, and to write as many letters and words as possible. The child who can write only three letters and recognize five words is seen to have strengths in being able to do so. That is, the *Reading Recovery* teacher does not say, "Well, we need to teach him (her) 23 more letters in the alphabet and 213 more words from the Dolch list." Rather, the intervention that follows (one-on-one tutoring for 30 minutes a day for 15 weeks) begins with two full weeks of "roaming around the known." Absolutely nothing new is taught during this time. The teacher *only* works with the child on what the child already knows, as demonstrated on the initial assessment. By the end of two weeks the child *knows* he or she is expert at least in some things. And the establishment of this belief — probably for the teacher as much as the student — is the basis for accelerating the student's reading development toward independence and competence. ESS demonstration schools are developing other examples of using assessment data to build on strengths and potential rather than simply identifying deficits.

Besides being used to inform teachers' interventions, assessment information should be used to reveal student strengths and potential, not just weaknesses.

Unfortunately, it is often possible for schools to change their curriculum and instructional practices faster than their assessment practices, simply because test and portfolio development can be complicated and time-consuming. Nevertheless, teachers must begin using performance-based assessments in their classrooms and proceed vigorously to implement reforms in curriculum and instruction for students at risk. Evidence shows that students taught in the ways advocated previously can still demonstrate substantial gains on traditional, discrete-point skills tests, although they may have learned the material in a meaning-centered, holistic, interactive mode. But these students will have to be oriented to the format and the protocols for taking such fill-in-the-bubble tests if they are to demonstrate their learning. As long as such tests are being used, educators should do everything they can to help each student not only to learn but also to succeed in whatever assessment will be used to judge that student. ❦

A
PREVENTIVE
APPROACH

In the Every Student Succeeds initiative, prevention takes precedence over remediation. Robert Slavin (1993) uses the analogy of children playing near a cliff as an ambulance and attendants wait below to save those who fall over the edge. He likens this scenario to that of categorical programs in their traditional role of remediating students after they have failed. Slavin suggests that in the past, rather than building a fence at the top of the cliff, we have relied on providing rescue equipment, rescue services, training of emergency personnel, and fiscal accountability for services.

Despite the effectiveness of a school's overall program, some students will inevitably experience severe difficulties resulting from chronic or acute circumstances. In these cases the goal is to intervene as early as possible to prevent the consequences from getting worse; that is, to build a fence at the top of the cliff. Slavin continues to use the term *remediation* but with a socially redeeming definition: an intervention that is intense, early, effective, and, therefore, short lived. In the context of the ESS initiative, we prefer to avoid the traditional connotations associated with *remediation* and replace it with *prevention*, at the same time including the qualities Slavin associated with the former.

For this initiative, prevention is viewed on a vertical continuum with two important levels, *primary* and *secondary*.

PRIMARY PREVENTION

Primary prevention involves providing high-quality, effective services in a way that might preclude the development of problems in the first place. It means closing the cracks in the core program so that fewer students fall through. Such prevention begins, in school at least, with giving all students opportunities for intensive interaction and success in a rich, meaning-centered curriculum and a safe and supportive environment. For the underachieving student this kind of curriculum and instruction will foster the development of basic and advanced skills within the context of authentic, meaningful activities. It will also generate student motivation that ensures each student's connectedness to school and the investment of energy necessary to engage, persist, and succeed. Primary prevention — a rich, meaning-centered core curriculum that builds on students' strengths — contrasts sharply with the more traditional approach of delivering a skills-based program to compensate for student deficits. Academic success in the core program, Element 1 in the ESS framework, is the foundation of the concept of primary prevention in kindergarten through grade twelve.

The early years of a child's learning career deserve special attention because they can be crucial to academic performance in kindergarten through grade twelve. The significance of these experiences makes it incumbent on staff in kindergarten through grade twelve to collaborate with staff in preschool programs whether located at one's school or not. Staff might begin by thinking of the early primary grades (preschool through grade three) as a unique segment to be developed and carried out collaboratively by all the adults involved. If, for example, *developmentally appropriate practices* are observed by teachers in these critical years, children can develop the love of learning, habits of mind, dispositions, and cognitive and metacognitive repertoire needed to be successful throughout the rest of their formal learning years. Learning an inventory of skills that are supposed to guarantee readiness is not enough.

Therefore, it is important to emphasize integrated thematic curriculum and assessment practices appropriate to each child's developmental level to promote self-esteem and positive learning outcomes. Teachers in preschool, kindergarten, and early primary grades must work together to examine their instructional practices so that students are exposed to coordinated, coherent, and high-quality programs from initial enrollment in school. Effective preschool programs, such as High/Scope, Head Start, the early primary program outlined in the Department's School Readiness Task Force report *Here They Come: Ready or Not,* and the Carpinteria Bilingual Preschool Program in California are excellent examples of primary prevention in the prekindergarten years. (See Resources, Appendix C.)

In addition, preschool and child development staff from latchkey programs should not be overlooked as a valuable resource for staff in elementary schools because they may be the first point of intake for the child and family. In addition, they often see the child and parents outside school hours, during vacations, and in off-track sessions for year-round schools. Often, other children in the same family are enrolled in these programs. When program staffs collaborate, a more complete family picture and intervention strategy is possible.

PREVENTION PAYS FUTURE DIVIDENDS

The predominant focus of nearly all of California's human service system is acute intervention, not prevention. However, all available evidence indicates that prevention and early intervention services are more successful than remediation educationally, socially, and economically. Increasingly, prevention is being credited with paying future dividends.

One preventive approach is preschool. For example, the Perry Preschool Project, conducted over a 20-year period by the High/Scope Educational Research Foundation in Ypsilanti, Michigan, demonstrated persuasively the cost-effectiveness of preschool programs for at-risk children from low-income families. For every dollar invested in the Perry Preschool, seven dollars were saved in other social and remediation costs over a period of time. Similarly, in 1988 the Commission for Economic Development published an analysis of the cost savings to business from quality child-care programs, and the California Business Roundtable and Association of California School Administrators recommended the expansion of preschool programs to support educational reform.

It has often been said that 80 percent of prison inmates are school dropouts. The costs involved are staggering. We spend only $4,000 to $5,000 per year to educate a child but $25,000 to $35,000 per year to incarcerate a convict. And these figures do not include the costs to the judicial and penal system in putting an individual behind bars and lost productivity and tax revenues. These and other studies have contributed to a growing awareness among policymakers and business leaders that the investment of resources in the preschool years and throughout a child's school years pays off in increased human capital and significant avoidance of costs for public social services later on. When any child loses in the system, *we all pay in one way or another; and to pay later is to pay an exceedingly higher price.*

OTHER POINTS OF PRIMARY PREVENTION

Primary prevention is not limited solely to early intervention for very young children; it can occur at several points within an individual's life span or during a student's educational career. For example, nearly 11 percent of the children born in California in 1988 were born to teenage parents, ranking the state first in the nation in teen pregnancies. The Teen Outreach Program sponsored by the Junior League has demonstrated that its model of health education and community service learning dramatically reduces pregnancies of participating middle grade and high school students —unlike the experiences of a similar group of nonparticipating students (Philliber, 1994). Prevention can also occur through prenatal care. An estimated 8 percent of surveyed teenage mothers received no prenatal care, even though for every dollar invested in prenatal care, $3.38 can be saved in the cost of care for low-birth-weight infants, who are at the greatest risk of developing serious disabilities.

Another stark example of the need for primary prevention is the current wave of children who were prenatally substance-exposed (e.g., "crack babies") and who exhibit a variety of behavioral and learning disorders that must now be addressed in the classroom. Schools should take action to coordinate services with the agencies that work with these infants, toddlers, preschoolers, and their families to ensure that every student enjoys a successful school experience.

SECONDARY PREVENTION AND INTERVENTION

The next level, *secondary prevention*, focuses on problems that have already begun to appear and interventions that will prevent a continuation of those problems. The problems may range from those that are relatively innocuous to those that are immobilizing or even life threatening. They may be academic or nonacademic, acute, or chronic. To handle such eventualities, the school must weave a safety net of processes, structures, roles, and services, both inside and outside the classroom, to ensure that no child is left behind.

Examples of problems at the lower end of the scale include attendance problems, a period of poor health or a hospitalization, the death of an important relative, and the loss of a friend whose family has moved away. At the upper end of the scale, more severe problems include the threat of suicide, chronic truancy, substance or alcohol abuse, malnutrition, illiteracy, chronic academic failure in one or more curriculum areas, homelessness, delinquency, racially motivated violence, and child abuse. The goal of prevention at this level is immediately to reduce the impact or duration of the problem and prevent future complications and their consequences. In these cases it is truly appropriate to speak about students' *needs*.

Glassbrook Elementary, a K-3 school in a high crime area of Hayward Unified School District, has hired a half-time social worker on staff who leads a Peace Club, conflict resolution, a family support group, and one-to-one counseling. Another function of the social worker is to handle crisis issues and extreme emergencies. (Far West Laboratory ESS Case Study, 1994)

ESS

However, secondary prevention refers to more than the amelioration of a problem. It means working back to the causes and eradicating the problem altogether. This perspective on prevention supports the central theme of Every Student Succeeds by suggesting that whatever is humanly possible is done to remove impediments — minor or severe — that stand in the way of each student's optimal academic, psychological, and social development.

Approaches to consider for improving a school's safety net capacity for secondary prevention are the following:

1. Developing a network of improved personal connections or relationships between each student and a variety of caring adults, encouraging all adults, no matter what their official job, to take on the role of caretaker and lookout

2. Developing organizational structures and processes in the school and district to support these connections as well as formal school site strategies

3. Involving the parents and the community in defined activities and programs to prevent or solve problems as they arise

4. Forming a local Healthy Start-type collaborative which would inventory available resources, assess community strengths and weaknesses, identify common goals, and begin by providing one or two high priority school-linked services

PERSONAL CONNECTIONS

The *first approach*, involving improved personal connections, requires that adults no longer simply act as purveyors of services to students as recipients. Adults are not just academic merchants with students as consumers. Rather, a school can establish practices and expectations that promote the kind of personal relationships and personal attention needed to prevent any student from being neglected or disconnecting in any way from school.

For teachers in particular, this concept falls under the heading of "teaching the child," not just "teaching the curriculum." Some feel that it is most difficult at the secondary level to focus enough on teaching the child because a strong bias often exists in favor of teaching one's subject in the departmentalized context of grades seven through twelve. *Caught in the Middle*, a document on middle-grade reform prepared by the Middle Grades Task Force, together with the recent high school practice

Secondary prevention refers to more than the amelioration of a problem. It means working back to the causes and eradicating the problem altogether.

Educators at the
elementary and
secondary levels are
encouraged to accept
the idea that "problems
with students" may be
"problems with the
system." Consequently,
solutions will begin to
be viewed as residing
more in how the school
responds to different
kinds of students rather
than in the students
themselves.

Cross-age tutoring helps Frank Paul Elementary
students in Alisal Union Elementary School District.

of dividing the school into "houses," offers recommendations for change in this direction in secondary schools. On the other hand, the child-centeredness of the elementary program may bias educators toward a focus on student needs (a term that is often a euphemism for student deficits), leading to the benevolent practice of unwittingly blaming the victim. Educators at the elementary and secondary levels are encouraged to accept the idea that "problems with students" may be "problems with the system." Consequently, solutions will begin to be viewed as residing more in how the school responds to different kinds of students rather than in the students themselves.

Practices consistent with this perspective can be as simple as teachers setting time aside daily to walk around the classroom and note how individual students are doing. A teacher might even create a private calendar to ensure personal contact with five or six different students each day. Classified staff might establish a priority interacting personally with students and observing problems or changes in students' behavior. Using dialogue journals in class, either written or recorded on tape, is a daily or weekly practice that can keep teachers in touch with their students' academic and personal lives at any grade level.

This approach requires every adult involved with a student to be responsible for that child's success in school and to alert others in the system at the first signs of trouble. Included are bus drivers, secretaries, food-service workers, custodians, groundskeepers, maintenance workers, volunteers, grounds supervisors, librarians, paraprofessionals, auxiliary personnel, teachers, administrators, and school volunteers. In a genuine school community, older students (including these educational levels) would also be given a role in mentoring and monitoring younger students to help flag problems as early as possible.

The approach described previously would help those in the school community begin to see themselves as front-line providers of counseling and guidance and as student advocates. For this expanded role all adults at the school will most likely need training. Specifically, teachers might be helped to recognize and support immigrant students who arrive with emotional trauma; be sensitive to cultural differences, language back-grounds, discrimination, and racism; be alert to peer pressure related to gangs, sex, drugs, and good grades; and recognize students having severe problems at home caused by violence, physical abuse, substance abuse, divorce, or poor nutrition.

In addition, an alarming increase in the number of students born with the effects of alcohol and illegal drugs requires that teachers and administrators be given specific help in learning how to handle the multiplicity of learning, emotional, and behavior problems that the students bring to school. Professional development may also include assistance in learning how to provide sheltered instruction in English for speakers of other languages; receiving training in TESA (Teacher Expecta-tions for Student Achievement) and GEESA (Gender and Ethnic Equity for Student Achievement); and learning techniques for promoting positive self-esteem and prosocial attitudes and behaviors, especially in the context of cooperative learning. (See Appendix C.)

Counseling and guidance services, as with other supplementary services, are best founded on advocacy for the strengths and potential of students who are at risk of school failure. These services can be made more personalized. And the adults in this service area can increase their impact by working closely with teachers, other specialists, parents, outside educational and social service agencies, and the students them-selves to facilitate the optimal progress of every student. Counselors may also broker services, mediate, counsel, schedule, advise, and assess. Most important, counselors must not ignore an obstacle in the path of a student's growth and future aspirations by supporting rigid decisions on homogeneous grouping and tracking based on the student's level of academic performance.

At the secondary level in particular, counselors can help develop school policies and procedures for encouraging as many students as possible to attempt more challenging course work while coordinating higher placements with teachers. Providing such students with extra support before, during, or after school, arranging for personalized help from tutors and mentors, setting up student study groups, and alerting parents to new demands being placed on a student in a more advanced course are all ways in which counselors can help students choose and succeed at more challenging paths through school than they or other adults might ordinarily expect are possible. And again, to be effective at all this, the counselors must be able to establish a personal relationship, however minimal, with each student.

PALS (People Assisting Learner Success) are adult volunteers matched to particular Almeria Middle School students who visit the student at school at least once a week. PALS assists students with difficult assignments, engage in social activities such as a sports events, provide informal counseling, or are there just to be part of the student's support network.
(Far West Laboratory ESS Case Study, 1994)

The primary focus of restructuring at Sanborn Elementary in East Salinas has been to create three teams of teachers and staff called minischools: Discovery Minischool, International Minischool of Arts and Sciences, and Community Minischool. The minischool staff, regular and special population teachers and support staff cooperate in planning curriculum, making budgetary decisions, and selecting professional development opportunities. The school leadership team is composed of two members from each minischool and two instructional aides. (Far West Laboratory ESS Case Study, 1994)

ORGANIZED STRUCTURES AND PROCESSES

The *second approach,* that of developing more formal school site structures and processes, might involve *Student Study Teams* (SSTs). These teams can play the dual role of personally addressing problems associated with individual students and influencing schoolwide practices to prevent future problems. An *advisory period* or *homeroom-type structure* in the middle grades can provide opportunities at the school site for teachers to play an effective caretaker role. In a middle school in San Diego, the homeroom teacher is charged with being each student's advocate. Whenever a student gets into trouble in another class, the student is referred to the homeroom teacher for counseling, mediation, or other help to solve the problem. This school structure and new teacher role has changed the "us-and-them" culture that so often characterizes the relationship between students and teachers in the middle grades.

Dividing the large high school into *"houses"* or *"schools-within-a-school"* helps secondary teachers and students develop supportive relationships. Such structures also increase the sensitivity of the system to identify students who begin to disconnect. Ungraded elementary configurations with the same teachers and students working together over a number of years can also build strong, caring relationships. An elementary school teacher in the Salinas Valley has experimented with a kindergarten through grade six ungraded classroom whose members are organized as a "functional family."

Study groups, cooperative learning groups, project groups, peer counseling, cross-age tutoring, and *student buddy systems* that are set up for newcomers are other examples of classroom structures that can provide critical support for the vulnerable student. A high school in Oakland provided a telephone in its media lab, where video and radio programs, photography, the school newspaper, and the school annual were produced. A student who was tardy or truant and responsible for a part of the school newspaper could be called at home by the student's teammates to make sure that a deadline was met — an example of positive peer pressure.

Cross-age tutoring is another important structure to help students with academic or attendance problems or both. The academic and social benefits have already been mentioned. Schools should set up such programs on a scale necessary to help significantly the students most in need. Students having academic problems or attendance problems are the first to be involved, as both tutors and tutees, and the involvement is daily whenever possible. As an added benefit, this strategy is extremely cost-effective in an era of tight budgets.

In this regard Rekrut (1994) states that:

Indeed, a meta-analysis by Levin, Glass, and Meister (1984) found that pupil-to-pupil tutoring was more effective as an instructional method per US $100 of cost per pupil than computer-aided instruction, reducing class size, increasing instructional time, and adult tutoring. The researchers observed that a traditional labor intensive method, cross-age tutoring, yielded a cost-effectiveness ratio nearly four times that of reducing class size and increasing instructional time. (p. 357)

And this practice is consistent with the community of inquiry recommended earlier whereby everyone in the school is both a teacher and a learner.

Other formal schoolwide structures or practices designed to ensure prevention at the secondary level might include the following:

1. Categorical program planning and monitoring teams
2. Regular briefing sessions between sending and receiving teachers as students move between grade levels; between schools or programs, such as preschool (private or public) and kindergarten; between alternative sites and the neighborhood school; between special education sites and the mainstream school or classrooms; and between latchkey, child care, or before- and after-school community tutorial programs
3. Up-to-date cumulative folders for each student — transferred electronically within the same district as needed
4. Parent conferences in which the explicit goal is not only to discuss academic progress but also to get acquainted personally with parents and students and capitalize on this information for improved classroom learning opportunities (The *California Learning Record* provides a vehicle to accomplish such goals)
5. Planned teacher-parent orientation and get-acquainted sessions
6. Planned participation by the school's adults in community activities, functions, and service programs or projects
7. A program of teacher and student volunteers in night school classes for high school graduation or ESL

PARENT AND COMMUNITY INVOLVEMENT

The *third approach* is to involve parents and community members more in the educational process. They are rich resources of knowledge, skills, influence, personnel, and material or financial help to the school. Solidarity can be built among adults to foster student success through informed and effective parent advisory committees; regular community meetings and in-home coffee klatches involving school personnel, parents, and community members volunteering in school or mentoring students; planned student visits; and service projects in the community.

Research on parent involvement (McLaughlin & Shields, 1987), especially for low-income parents, indicates that parents can have a significant positive impact on their children's academic achievement but often do not. Among the reasons for this shortcoming are educators' belief systems and schools' policies on parent involvement, which, in effect, block the effective involvement of parents. A study of reform conducted in an inner-city Los Angeles school (Goldenberg & Gallimore, 1991) revealed that bilingual educators did not believe that their students' parents could or would help in developing Spanish literacy. After all, many were illiterate or worked long hours. As a result of staff development, however, the educators found not only that these parents *would* but that, when instructed, they certainly *could* assist competently, bringing about significant positive gains in their children's reading achievement in Spanish. The key to effective parent involvement seems to be to *involve parents mostly on their terms,* not just on the school's (McLaughlin & Shields, 1987). *Terms* include *time, place, agenda,* and *language.* The school that capitalizes on parent power will be the school to heed this important premise.

The community at large is the other major source of support in the third approach. To solve potentially serious problems as they arise, the school needs established connections with the health and social services available in the community, including, at a minimum, a list of all available sources of help inside and outside the school and school district. A personal relationship between someone at the school — the principal, a resource teacher, or community liaison — and those agencies can do much to facilitate timely service. The school, with the assistance of the district and county offices of education, needs to have the capacity to broker such services when needed. Administrators, teachers, and parents need this resource information if they are to get immediate professional help necessary to prevent social, emotional, or health problems from becoming barriers to student success. Element 3 deals with how a school as an institution might redefine its role to address student health and social service needs when those needs overwhelm the one or two persons in a school that might broker such community services. The Healthy Start model is presented as a strategy for providing comprehensive integrated school-linked services to children and their families.

RESEARCH ON RESILIENCY

Finally, no discussion of prevention would be complete without a review of the contributions of research on *resiliency*. This topic fits under both primary and secondary prevention strategies and involves *the entire school community, the home, the child's peers,* and *the community at large*. We all know too clearly what risk factors many of our students face. Such negative influences as drugs, sex, fads, the media, broken homes, crime, negative peer pressure, discrimination or racism, lack of supervision, inappropriate or nonexistent role models, mental and physical abuse, mental illness, poverty, homelessness, and environmental pollution plague far too many children. These children are lucky to make it to school at all — let alone learn.

The good news from the research on resiliency is that *a majority of children* exposed consistently to such negative influences as alcoholism, child abuse, crime, drugs, and mental illness *do not* succumb to these problems (Benard, 1991). They seem to be resilient or, to some degree, are buffered by protective influences or factors that help them develop successfully and go on to make positive contributions to society as adults. In light of these hopeful examples, questions for educators are: How do we maximize each child's chances of surviving and developing optimally in spite of such negative factors in the child's life? How do we help our students become resilient? How do we provide them the necessary buffers of protection in a hostile environment?

A West Randall Elementary School student practices his penmanship. (Fontana Unified School District)

Benard (1991) has summarized the protective factors important to helping children be resilient in the face of negative influences. Needless to say, these factors go well beyond admonishing children to just say "No." She organizes the factors into the four domains in the following chart.

Four Domains of Resiliency
(Benard, 1991)

COMMUNITY	FAMILY
Clear norms for families and schools	*Religious affiliation*
Clear rules and regulations	*Consistent rituals and traditions*
Intergenerational ties	*Clear rules and regulations*
Competent role models	*Domestic responsibilities*
External support systems	*Significant relationship with parent or caregiver*
CHILD AND PEERS	**SCHOOL**
Ability to set goals	*Clear rules and regulations*
Good sense of humor	*Competent role models*
Autonomy	*Great expectations for all children*
Ability to develop friendships	*Social competencies*
Strong sense of the future	*Relationship with significant adult*
Strong social competencies	*Goal-directed behavior*
Belief in one's self	*School ethos (values)*
Good health	
Easy temperament	

Because almost every school in the state enrolls some children at risk, the adults at school should begin to factor in to their roles and work plans ways to address the points outlined previously. How many need to be in place for each child is unclear. In some cases of successful resilience, it was just one. We must first look for children who may have few to none of these protective factors working in their lives. The concept of resiliency promises to be a fruitful area of investigation and program design. ❧

INTEGRATED TOTAL PROGRAM FOR EACH STUDENT, WITH A PERSONAL TOUCH

This section provides an overview of three major areas related to an integrated total program for each student. The first area involves the organization and delivery of educational services within the school, especially in terms of categorical programs. The goal here is to coordinate the program for each individual student so that it is coherent and effective. The second area relates to parent and community linkages that coordinate with the school within its larger context. Because the larger context of the home and community can have strong influences on student performance in school, any framework that does not involve such linkages as a central feature of the program will be deprived of the indispensable help needed to support a successful educational experience for each child. The third area relates to coordinated health and social services.

ORGANIZATION AND DELIVERY OF SERVICES

The objective of this element is to develop an integrated, coordinated program of supplementary services for every student, including the coordination of such services with each other and with the core program. To do so, classroom teachers must assume a stronger decision-making role in the education of their multifunded students than is commonly done. In addition, parent and community involvement to support students' academic successes must be increased.

Coordinating all of a student's services so that they are comprehensive and coherent is an important goal, especially for the multifunded student receiving help from such funding sources as the School Improvement Program (SIP), Economic Impact Aid/Limited-English-Proficient Student Funds, Chapter 1, and Migrant Education, a speech therapist, and a resource specialist. All adults that "share" the same students should meet regularly and systematically to ensure a seamless program of services for each child by name.

A note of caution is in order before proceeding with this important concept of integration and coordination of services. Although necessary, this kind of coordination is not a panacea if the school has not reasonably reformed its academic program in accordance with Element 1. It may do little good to mainstream special education students more effectively and carry out side-by-side collaborative teaching in a classroom in which a continuum of skills and bits of knowledge are taught directly to homogeneous groups of low-performing students. Nor is it sufficient, for example, to solve a culturally diverse student's home or health problems only, thereby clearing the way for that student to participate in a program in which similar students without such problems are failing anyway.

The section that follows describes a two-level model for the effective coordination, integration, and delivery of supplementary services at the school site. The first level addresses the school's capacity to provide *comprehensive* or schoolwide supplementary services meaningfully to students and in a coordinated manner. The second level addresses the *specific* problems of students who may still fail to be served by such a planned system or who may experience unique or acute difficulties at some time in their school careers.

COMPREHENSIVE, COORDINATED SUPPLEMENTARY SERVICES

Planning and monitoring the day-to-day program of supplementary services can best be accomplished when all adults who work with multifunded students meet with each other formally and regularly. To do so requires finding time to conduct the meetings. The purpose of such meetings is to coordinate activities focusing on the "shared" multifunded students. This group would include all specialists, classroom teachers of the students, and appropriate adults outside the school, such as preschool and latchkey-program providers and those who may work in community tutorial or child development programs.

These adults will need time to engage in systemic planning at the beginning of the year. They might, for example, bring together their lists of identified students in order to plan services for any students they might have in common. This planning may be the collaborative development of individualized learning plans for each student receiving supplementary services. Staff might then establish agreements on how they formally communicate with each other daily, or at least weekly, on the content and outcomes of their respective services, such as through brief lesson plans or summaries on NCR forms, before or after school meetings, in Student Study Teams meetings for selected students, and so forth. (See further for a discussion of Student Study Teams.)

At Carr Intermediate School, Santa Ana Unified School District, with 68% of students having limited-English proficiency, 63% of the support staff are bilingual and 41% of the teachers have a specialized credential or language certification. (Far West Laboratory ESS Case Study, 1994)

They could also, perhaps in cooperation with or under the supervision of a school-site or district administrator, periodically monitor their services and student progress as well as carry out an end-of-year process and product evaluation of their work. In all of their decisions, however, these adults must treat supplementary services as a means to a common end: *to enrich* students' opportunities to participate in the core program. These safety-net strategies and services may involve "pull-outs." Admittedly, pull-outs have often been damaging to students by stigmatizing them or preventing them from having access to a rich core curriculum by substituting a more sterile, watered-down one delivered by staff less trained than the classroom teacher. However, "push-in" programs can suffer from exactly the same shortcomings in spite of their delivery within the classroom. What counts in providing supplementary services, then, is not the location of services but their content, intent, duration, effectiveness, relation to the core program, and nature of the coordination and compensation for what is missed in class.

For example, Reading Recovery is a pull-out one-to-one tutoring service. But students not being pulled out consistently want to know when it will be their turn, and most participants are back in class for reading as well as their peers within 15 to 16 weeks.

STUDENT-SPECIFIC SUPPLEMENTARY SERVICES

Staff might also develop at the beginning of the year a system or model to help any student who may not be served by the core or supplementary service programs. The model would include a process for student identification (a "flagging system"), delivery of service, and the criteria and mechanism for release or discontinuation of services. It would serve students who develop unique problems not easily handled in the course of the core program or through the normal day-to-day coordinated and integrated delivery of supplementary services.

These services represent agreed-on resources that staff at the school know about and can take advantage of as needed. Any of these services might include the principal and the following:

1. The classroom teacher as the initial person to intervene to try to solve any problem that might arise (If the problem cannot be solved between the teacher, student, and, perhaps, the parents, the teacher assumes the role of broker and, eventually, manager of services to the student beyond the classroom.)
2. The teacher and a grade-level mentor, lead, or key teacher
3. The teacher and available specialist(s) at the school district or county

What counts in providing supplementary services, then, is not the location of services but their content, intent, duration, effectiveness, relation to the core program, and nature of the coordination and compensation for what is missed in class.

4. The teacher, available specialist(s), and the Student Study Teams (SST)

5. The teacher, the SST, and the individualized education program team (Radius & Lesniak, 1988) as appropriate

This model must not, legally or practically, be implemented rigidly. To ensure that students are not arbitrarily prevented from receiving necessary services, especially those offered through special education, several operating conditions must be placed on such a system.

For example, students should be able to enter or exit the system at any level of service; staff should be able to decide when student performance warrants a particular service configuration; and parents should be informed and their comments sought on student assessments, the consideration of providing supplementary services, and the nature of the services to be provided. Finally, and perhaps most importantly, arbitrary steps or time limits should not be allowed to become barriers to students' receipt of appropriate services as quickly as possible and for as long as they need them. With these flexibilities any student having difficulties in school should be able to receive appropriate services as close to the classroom program as possible, from the best qualified staff, and as soon as possible. Without such systemic options staff are often required to cast about for help or keep problems to themselves. With official structures and procedures as options, staff members have legitimate and ready-made ways of getting help for students every time a need arises.

In ESS the Student Study Teams figures prominently in the Secondary Prevention services described previously. As an important school structure and process, it must often take on two functions. As such, it can be referred to as the Student Study Team Plus (SST+). The SST carries out the diagnosis and planning for improving an individual student's performance and can also periodically make recommendations to the school, such as through the school's Leadership Team, to improve schoolwide policies and practices related to recurring problems that may jeopardize the success of some students.

If, for example, a significant number of immigrant children are being referred for problems with reading English, the SST+ might recommend that the school look into its program of English-language development and criteria for the introduction of English reading to non-native speakers of English. Or if a number of students have been referred in the middle grades for having academic problems as a result of extensive peer pressure to do badly in school, the SST might alert the Leadership Team to consider ways of encouraging peer-supported norms of academic excellence.

PERSONAL CONNECTIONS

A discussion on developing improved personal connections and relationships between students and adults at school is provided on pp. 55–57.

PARENT AND COMMUNITY LINKAGES

Parent and family support, involvement, and a sense of connection with their children's schooling are indispensable for the success of any student, especially for those considered most at risk. Evidence exists that involvement of parents is extremely helpful in raising the performance levels of students at risk regardless of a student's socioeconomic background. The basis for a school's effectiveness with these parents lies, however, in how educators get parents involved *on parents' terms* rather than on the school's terms exclusively. It is important to connect parents not only for their official programmatic "responsibilities" but also for their children's performance and satisfaction — not to mention their hopes for their children's success.

Many commercially prepared programs provide parent education and involvement training packages and process strategies. School district and school staff must identify with parents in their community what the needs and priorities will be each year and evaluate the available prepared programs or Department models and materials recommended. A policy adopted by the California State Board of Education contains the recommended criteria against which any parent program can be measured.

The adopted policy outlines six types of involvement that comprehensive parent involvement programs should be designed to:

1. Help parents develop parenting skills and foster conditions at home that support learning.
2. Provide parents with knowledge of techniques designed to assist children in learning at home.
3. Provide access to and coordinate community and support services for children and families.
4. Promote clear two-way communication between the school and the family as to the school programs and children's progress.
5. Involve parents, after appropriate training, in instruction and support roles at school.
6. Support parents as decision makers and develop their leadership in governance, advisory, and advocacy roles.

"The mission of parent involvement programs is to promote increased student academic success by facilitating the development and implementation of comprehensive, continuing family-community-school partnership in all California schools."
— California Strategic Plan for Parental Involvement in Education

The federal Even Start program and a variety of family literacy models throughout the state provide the kind of support parents need to get effectively involved in their children's education and help themselves educationally as well. In this regard the Megaskills (Rich, 1992) training program, a national model, is ideal for comprehensively training parents to be able to perform all of the above roles and functions by helping them first become more powerful and effective parents to their children. Megaskills training helps to develop habits of effective parents and students including confidence, motivation, effort, responsibility, initiative, perseverance, caring, teamwork, common sense, and problem solving.

Less-structured interventions can become part of the school culture to help the system make better use of all human and material resources. For example, staff can be alert to parental strengths and interests and involve parents in supporting classroom activities, student programs, and presentations. Educators can meet parents in their homes or in the community, not just at school, and at times that are most convenient for parents. Such meetings can be initiated by educators with no defined purpose other than to help the community and school to get to know each other as people and to establish a relationship of trust and mutual interest for future collaborations. Holding coffee klatches in homes or meetings in community centers, participating in community events and organizations, accessing parents in adult classes, providing training important to parents both on site and off site (e.g., in parenting, teaching literacy or English as a second language, accessing social services, nutrition, consumer education) can all be effective ways of interacting with parents on their terms for the benefit of their children's success in school.

Community involvement can be a rich source of support for a school trying to confront the difficult task of providing an effective program for each student and with limited resources. For example, older students, including college and university students, retired adults and other volunteers, such as adults in local business and industry, could be actively involved before, during, after school, or on weekends in tutoring, counseling, mentoring, and supporting students at risk. Such programs of involvement could reduce the student-to-adult ratio, which often reaches 500 to 1 for public school counselors or 30-40 to 1 for elementary teachers and 150-180 to 1 for secondary teachers. In comparison with the effectiveness of personal contact, all other institutional, "remote-control" forms of intervention and support are often much less powerful.

Private, nonprofit organizations and universities can work with the schools to ensure that students at risk (1) understand their opportunities for work and higher education; (2) understand the standards to be met to take advantage of those opportunities; and (3) are provided the tutoring and support necessary to meet those standards. An example of an innovative, collaborative program directed to a specific student population is the HAWK Project at San Francisco State University, which is working with three school districts to address the problems of African American males.

Students at risk benefit from community counseling services.

But help does not have to go in just one direction — from the community to the school. The relationship can be mutually supportive and can give students a role in serving, thereby helping them to promote their self-worth, pride, and dignity as well as a better sense of connection between their learning in school and life. Students who are at risk can be organized to contribute to the community through such service activities as the following:

1. Students, adult, and community volunteers, with school and agency staff, restore creeks, watersheds, and riparian habitats as part of science classes.
2. In English classes, students write about their experiences working in homeless shelters, hospitals, homes for the elderly, and preschools and discuss similar issues found in literature.
3. K–12 youth are trained as tutors for younger children in curriculum subjects; docents to serve in museums, historical community buildings and natural habitats; facilitators in conflict resolution; and peer helpers to improve safety in their schools and communities and to work with HIV/AIDS and drug abuse prevention.
4. Students learn about local community institutions, organizations, and public policies as they perform service activities linked to their study of social studies and history.

When these experiences are integrated into the school curriculum, they are called service learning. Such programs may have positive effects on overall school performance of students at risk and reduce truancy and dropout rates, as in San Antonio's cross-age tutoring program for Hispanic students at risk.

But help does not have to go in just one direction — from the community to the school. The relationship can be mutually supportive and can give students a role in serving, thereby helping them to promote their self-worth, pride, and dignity as well as a better sense of connection between their learning in school and life.

COORDINATED HEALTH AND SOCIAL SERVICES

A broader mission for schools is necessary if the variety of services children receive are to be coordinated better and oriented more toward prevention. This broader mission does not imply that schools will provide services within the purview of other public or private human service agencies. Rather, it suggests that schools take the initiative in developing collaborative partnerships with mental health, health, juvenile justice, and social service agencies on behalf of their students and in coordination with their families. Included would be a provision of on-site space for youth service providers from other agencies or facilitation of coordinated service delivery to students and families.

In elementary schools and secondary schools throughout the state, health and social services are being provided or at least brokered by social workers and health professionals on campus. The Healthy Start Initiative (S.B. 620/1991) provides great opportunities for schools, districts, and county offices of education to provide comprehensive, integrated school-linked services using the schools as the hub for service integration. The goal of Healthy Start is to produce measurable improvements in outcomes for children and families by providing integrated health, mental health, social, educational, and other support services.

Healthy Start is a competitive grant program that allows schools, in partnership with public and private service providers, to develop unique service provision plans based on assessed needs and strengths of the communities they will serve. Healthy Start funds are targeted to schools with high populations of low-income and limited-English-proficient students. Elementary, middle, and high schools may apply. Schools are not expected to provide the necessary services, but rather they become the location where services are provided by appro-

Coordinated services benefit students at Carver Elementary School, San Diego City Unified School District.

priate professionals. Children and families are more likely to use convenient services connected with the neighborhood school.

The key components of successful local Healthy Start implementation include designing culturally and linguistically appropriate services; providing case-managed services for students and families that are most in need; including parents in the development and implementation of the local initiative as active decision makers; and, utilizing primary or informal supports such as neighborhood groups, law enforcement, recreational facilities, and community organizations thereby lessening the need for more formal and costly services. Healthy Start initiatives shift the focus to prevention by devising comprehensive strategies that span the continuum from primary prevention through crisis intervention and follow-through.

The support services that are being offered to meet the needs of Healthy Start students and families include educational (tutoring, dropout prevention); mental health and counseling (support groups, therapy, substance abuse); medical and health (vision, hearing, dental, Child Health and Disabilities Service, acute care, preventive health, nutrition); basic needs (food, clothing, shelter, transportation); family support (child protection, parenting education, child care); employment (career counseling, job training, and placement); recreational; and income maintenance (Medi-Cal, Aid to Families with Dependent Children, food stamps). Currently, 112 operational grants are providing services in 372 schools in urban, suburban, and rural communities throughout the state. Also, 226 planning grants involving 588 schools are in progress.

Although a school or cluster of schools may not be able to implement a comprehensive program without grant assistance, it is possible to move forward and, perhaps, provide one or two key services. Schools, districts, and county offices of education can begin by bringing collaborative partners from key agencies and community programs on board and learn from one another about how the health, mental health, and social services operate in the community. It is important to build a constituency by getting parents, community and agency staff, and school and district staff involved. Then, community strengths and needs should be assessed; parents and families are asked what they need. It is helpful to find out what local collaboratives and initiatives are already in the community and coordinate the school's efforts. Informal supports may be utilized throughout the community. When it is possible, only one formal service component is pilot-tested. For example, a county mental health worker is stationed one day a week at the school.

Healthy Start shifts the focus from intervention to prevention and strives for measurable improvements in such areas as school readiness, academic success, health and mental health, and family functioning. Schools and their collaborative partners work together to provide comprehensive school-linked integrated services, including preventive health services, mental health and counseling services, academic tutoring and dropout prevention, career counseling, parenting education, and child abuse prevention services. (CDE Staff Report, 1994)

Promising models of interagency coordination at the regional or county level in California and nationally should also be nurtured and studied carefully. California has a number of counties that have implemented multiagency models (e.g., San Francisco County's Teenage Pregnancy and Parenting Project, Ventura County's Children's Mental Health Project, San Bernardino County's Children's Network, First Fund of Children's Resources, and California's Early Start Program — IDEA, Part H). These established models could provide valuable information and technical assistance support to other California cities and counties considering similar planning and implementation projects. Additionally, S.B. 997 (Presley-Brown) encourages the development of countywide comprehensive children's services coordination projects.

The Healthy Kids, Healthy California initiative, sponsored by the Department of Education since 1989, encourages schools, school districts, and county offices of education to enlist broad-based community support in the development of comprehensive health programs in each school. An important component of Healthy Kids, Healthy California is the Department's goal of eliminating usage of drugs, alcohol, and tobacco on school campuses. The Department's guidelines call for schools, school districts, and county offices of education to establish formal partnerships with parents, community leaders, and local information, treatment, and law enforcement agencies to coordinate their resources in the development of a collaborative prevention program aimed at the use of drugs, alcohol, and tobacco.

Programs that have long recognized the importance of considering the whole child (including nutrition, health, and social services needs) in the educational process include pregnant and teenage parenting programs; early childhood development programs, such as parent/infant education programs, private preschools, child development programs, state preschool programs, and Head Start programs; latchkey programs; and the Cities in Schools Program. A comprehensive program must be built to address each child's emotional, social, and physical development in addition to cognitive development. ESS suggests that this approach be incorporated into programs at all levels, from preschool through grade twelve. 🍎

EFFECTIVE STAFF DEVELOPMENT

4

Much can be gained by a staff focusing its energies on a limited number of ambitious goals, improving its organization, and changing its policies in a variety of areas. At some point, however, improved learning for the most diverse and challenging populations of students in California requires improved teaching among the individuals who work with those students day-to-day. And improving instructional skills in the classroom requires effective staff development. It is the major formal vehicle for bringing new information into a school community and getting the members to process it and apply it in their daily work. In short, it is a way to break the status quo of unrealized potential for many of the adults and students in our most challenging schools and communities.

INCLUDING ALL STAKEHOLDERS IN CONTINUING EDUCATION

At first glance, *staff development* may not appear to be the most appropriate term to describe this activity of lifelong learning for adults in charge of educating children. By definition it limits participation to official "staff" only. Yet ensuring dramatic improvements in educational outcomes for children most at risk often requires that all stakeholders — certificated and classified employees, parents, retirees, members of the business community, and even students themselves — improve their educational know-how through some kind of in-service program. The alternative, *professional development* is appropriate for certificated staff but by implication also leaves out many people who are not considered formally a part of the educational profession. Training is more generic and has been criticized as inadequate because of its demeaning connotations to the professional status of teachers. In addition, it seems too shallow for the kind of in-depth, ongoing, and multifaceted activities that characterize the best in in-service training for teachers.

Carr Intermediate School believes that ongoing, preferably in-house, staff development is the key to bringing about and sustaining the successes of restructuring. Administration and a Project Specialist coordinate a comprehensive program of staff development that first focuses on the process of change by developing staff awareness about alternative paradigms and new ways of thinking and working together. (Far West Laboratory ESS Case Study, 1994)

To solve this dilemma, we fall back on the term staff development but redefine staff to mean any adult or student who participates in any type of in-service training program designed to improve student results at a given school. In short, any individual, to the degree that he or she plays a role in educating children, is considered *staff*. Included are individuals such as teachers, cross-age tutors, intergenerational volunteers, bus drivers, paraprofessionals, food-service workers, and administrators.

DETERMINING CONTENT

The content of staff development activities is the first important consideration in developing an effective program. One guiding principle for deciding on what to include is to have the participants themselves participate fully in deciding on what they need to know. This approach, often attempted by means of a one-time, comprehensive staff development survey administered to the faculty, is not, however, the most effective way to begin.

A better approach is for the school community to take time out initially to collect data, both qualitative and quantitative, on how students are faring at the school. This information should include, at a minimum, students' academic performance across time in the various subject areas of the curriculum. The data should also be disaggregated by student population, (e.g., ethnicity; gender; limited-English-proficient, fluent-English-proficient, English only; categorical programs; grade level; classroom). Problems in learning revealed in a school community's analysis of such data are a sound starting point for determining who and what might be included in a staff development program.

Before final decisions on staff development are made, however, a focus area or areas need to be agreed on. Research on the successful institutionalization of effective educational innovations indicates that the most successful reform projects include a limited number of ambitious initiatives (Rand, 1978). Focus areas might include reading, science, mathematics, cooperative learning, bilingual program design, parent involvement, and integrated thematic instruction. Care must be taken, however, not to undertake only to develop in-service training programs involving first order changes in the focus area (i.e., changes that represent improvements or refinements of current practice). Such changes rarely result in dramatic improvements in academic outcomes. Rather, it would be more powerful to commit to a few ambitious second order changes (i.e., replacing current "good" practices with "better" or "best" practices) (Cuban, 1988).

Once the major agreements or commitments are made that define a school's reform focus, a subcommittee of the stakeholders needs time to review research and current promising practices related to the chosen focus area(s). This can be accomplished through the study of research summaries in the educational literature related to the focus area and by consulting educational experts, attending conferences, visiting other schools and each other's classrooms, and formally drawing on the expertise of existing staff.

Suppose, for example, a school chose reading as a major focus area, with the goal that each student by name be able to read at grade level or better in English or a home language other than English before graduating from the school. Such a choice would give the school clear direction for its staff development program. After appropriate study a staff development committee might agree to second order changes whereby daily vocabulary drills, lessons on grammar and punctuation, and round robin reading of the core works would be replaced by extensive free voluntary reading; a schoolwide reading campaign; writers' workshop; a combination of individual, shared, guided, and paired reading involving cross-age tutors or intergenerational volunteers; and a new performance-based assessment system in language arts. A staff development program could then be designed to help put such second order language arts changes into practice.

Students at Frank Paul Elementary School help each other with cross-age tutoring. (Alisal Union Elementary School District)

The eclectic nature of the traditional staff development survey cannot offer the power of focus, educational validity, ownership, and follow-through that the approach previously described can have. That approach guarantees not only that the participants in any staff development program have an effective voice but that the participants are as informed as possible before any substantial investment of money, time, and energy is made to learn new things.

A STAFF DEVELOPMENT MODEL FOR ENSURING SUFFICIENT FOLLOW-THROUGH

The model or protocol for conducting staff development is the next important consideration. Bruce Joyce and Beverly Showers (1987, 1988) have studied whether the kinds of activities selected in a staff development program have an effect on whether what is learned by the participants is transferred to the classroom and, more importantly, if they have any appreciable effect on student learning. Their research has been outlined and reinforced by Margarita Calderon, a bilingual staff development expert, who has studied and effectively applied their model in California for more than a decade. On the following table Calderon summarizes the effects on learning and on the transfer of training of that learning to the classroom within a four-point framework (Joyce & Showers, 1988; Showers, Joyce, & Bennett, 1987):

ACTIVITY	KNOWLEDGE & UNDERSTANDING	ABILITY TO USE NEW SKILL	TRANSFER TO CLASSROOM REPERTOIRE
Theory	90%	25%	5%
Demonstration	90%	50%	5%
Practice and Feedback	90%	90-95%	5%
Coaching or Collegial Support Meetings	95-100%	95-100%	90%

Virtually no transfer of training and, therefore, no effect on children's learning occurs unless the fourth activity, coaching or collegial support meetings, is included in the staff development program. Although most teachers have sat through a conference workshop of theory or perhaps even a demonstration of a strategy and have planned to put what they have learned into practice in their classroom within the week, they usually do not. Such a lack of transfer of training occurs for a variety of reasons, not the least of which are the obstacles of teacher isolation, uncooperative students, and lack of assistance when the first attempts are unsuccessful.

The speech and language specialist teams with the classroom teacher in a language arts activity. (Sacramento City Unified School District)

Peer coaching or, for teachers uncomfortable with venturing into such a practice right away, collegial support meetings provide the stimulation and support necessary to overcome such obstacles. Only then can teachers achieve what Joyce and Weil (1986) have called *executive control* of a strategy. The teacher can implement the components of a strategy or activity and modify, pace, or vary the strategy to fit a given learning situation, topic, or group of students. Joyce (1990) reports on research that shows that teachers who use a given strategy at the level of executive control achieve student gains of 1.0 or more standard deviations higher than teachers who use the strategy correctly but at a more mechanical level of implementation. Mechanical and executive control are rarely achieved without substantial follow-through activities in an ongoing staff development program. From this research it is clear that to get teachers to transfer their learning at a mechanical level into the classroom is ineffective. At some point executive control must be achieved for maximum gains to be realized.

To be effective, follow-through coaching activities should probably occur once or twice a month. Teachers can be organized into pairs or trios to serve as peer coaches for each other. Enlisting the help of a resource teacher, administrator, counselor, kindergarten teacher, or teacher on prep time or hiring a roving substitute for a couple of days a month are ways of releasing teachers to visit each other once every two weeks. A visit might last as little as 20 minutes — just enough time to observe a particular strategy or lesson. Each visit, preceded by a meeting to agree on what is to be observed, is followed by a meeting for feedback. The feedback — especially until the teacher partners build confidence with each other — should be as objective and descriptive as possible of the teachers' or students' behaviors relative to the activity or strategy under study. Even giving a higher proportion of positive to negative responses may not work as well initially as simply describing what was seen without placing a value on it. Asking questions to clarify or stimulate a colleague's thinking can also be effective.

To be effective, follow-through coaching activities should probably occur once or twice a month. Teachers can be organized into pairs or trios to serve as peer coaches for each other. Enlisting the help of a resource teacher, administrator, counselor, kindergarten teacher, or teacher on prep time or hiring a roving substitute for a couple of days a month are ways of releasing teachers to visit each other once every two weeks.

At no time should the feedback meeting serve the purpose of teacher evaluation and should probably not be conducted by an administrator. Instead, the goal is to have the teacher observed feel that this is a safe, risk-taking, learning experience. One of the best examples of such a model of peer coaching is to be found in the TESA program mentioned previously. It follows the four-stage model advocated by Joyce and Showers, including theory/awareness, modeling, practice/feedback, and peer coaching. As a variation on peer coaching in schools where such an activity is not yet a reality, teachers can turn on a tape recorder or even a portable video camera during a given activity and coach themselves on prearranged criteria or instructional features as they review the tape later at their leisure.

If participants choose to have collegial support meetings rather than engage in peer coaching, the meetings should be set up at least biweekly, with agendas that provide time to talk about specific, agreed-on strategies or activities that have been tried in class or are planned for the following week. Typically, the discussion should revolve around successes, problems, student reactions, the effectiveness of materials, suggested modifications in the strategy or activity, upcoming plans for implementing a new strategy or principle, and so on. Care must be taken that such meetings do not degenerate into a forum for "war stories," gripes, social chatter, or other unrelated concerns. The meeting should be devoted exclusively to improving one's craft.

Time is obviously a crucial factor in any effective staff development program that involves the kind of preparation, implementation, and follow-through described previously. If they are identified as School-Based Coordination Programs, schools legally have up to eight student-free days available for staff development at the decision of the local governing board. The days off cost the district nothing because average daily attendance is computed as if students were in attendance on those days. In year-round schools the eight days may be taken at the beginning, during, or at the end of the school year and throughout the calendar year. With a state waiver one school even distributed the days over 34 weeks in 90-minute planning and staff development periods (GAO, 1994). Whatever the final arrangement, the schools most in need of improvement (i.e., schools in crisis) should have as many of these days as possible made available to them, especially in the initial stages of change. Only in this way will the schools have a fighting chance of improving dramatically in both staff know-how and student outcomes as soon as possible.

Time is obviously a crucial factor in any effective staff development program that involves the kind of preparation, implementation, and follow-through.

Another option, which can be used in conjunction with the eight days, involves the extension of the teaching day by 15 to 20 minutes per day for four days a week and consequent reduction of teaching time by this accumulated amount one day a week. This strategy or variations on it have already been used by many schools in California to garner time for planning and staff development. Such a scheme would be one way to emulate the enviable situation that Stevenson and Stigler (1992) report for Chinese and Japanese teachers, who spend more time daily in school than American teachers (approximately 9.5 hours versus 7.5 hours) but less time with students (approximately 4 hours versus 6 hours). Specifically, teachers in Beijing spend only three hours per day with students. Much of the nonstudent time, however, (approximately 40 percent of their day) is spent in collegial support meetings — planning and reviewing curriculum and instruction in order to perfect their lessons.

NECESSITY OF ADMINISTRATIVE SUPPORT AND ONGOING DEVELOPMENT

Effective staff development has several important characteristics. It should involve all relevant stakeholders in planning, be focused on a limited number of ambitious second order change initiatives, and include sufficient follow-through to ensure effective implementation and subsequent student gains. A crucial point is that the follow-through involving coaching visits or collegial support meetings occur regularly each month and become a natural part of the school culture — as natural as faculty meetings, collecting milk money, bell schedules, or daily bulletins. The role of the school administration is vital to ensuring that such a staff development model, from start to finish, is carried out effectively. Budgets, schedules, arranging for substitutes and meeting times all require ongoing site-level if not district-level support. And it is the principal's constant reinforcement of a norm of risk-taking, experimentation, learning and implementing more powerful practices, and a focus on student achievement that will ensure that staff development will have the impact intended. One important gesture that a principal can make, especially found to be effective at the elementary level, is to attend all the staff development sessions as well (McLaughlin & Marsh, 1978).

The model described previously has been successfully applied with the help of cross-age tutors who work four days a week and debrief every Friday. In addition, parents help their children improve their reading and writing at home, and classified staff or volunteers work on campaigns to promote dramatic increases in reading for every student in school.

Almeria Middle School's principal has built a sense of community among the teachers. He's the driving force behind their readily sharing materials and ideas. Staff congratulate each other with "Almeri-Grams" and "Spout It Out" messages at staff meetings in which teachers are encouraged to step out of their comfort zone and explore new experiences and feelings. (Far West Laboratory ESS Case Study, 1994)

Physical science projects get serious attention at Azusa High School, Azusa Unified School District.

The sense of efficacy (McLaughlin & Marsh, 1978) for the participants in such a learning program is contagious. It also helps to change both adults' and students' attitudes about their potential for success when they see improved learning as a result of improved classroom strategies and activities. This phenomenon, attitudinal change and increased motivation as a result of successful teaching strategies, should not be underestimated as an important factor in making a struggling school community more than the sum of its parts and eventually an exemplary program. Indeed, effective staff development is one way to change school culture and help a school community achieve the metaphor of a center or community of inquiry (Joyce, 1990), in which everyone successfully develops as both a learner and a teacher.

California is fortunate to have a staff development infrastructure that supports many if not all of the aspects of powerful staff development described above. The California Subject Matter Projects for each of the curricular areas offer summer institutes that typically involve a number of follow-up collegial support sessions for up to two years after each summer institute. Teachers frequently describe such staff development experiences as transformational. Follow-up is also a feature of the California School Leadership Academy, a three-year training program for administrators in all aspects of effective schooling. ❧

ESS

ELEMENT

5
PLANNING, IMPLEMENTING, AND EVALUATING THE TOTAL SCHOOL PROGRAM

Processes and structures need to be established to plan, implement, and evaluate the school's program for improving its performance with students at risk. It is important to have the following:

1. A vision — not just a mission, goals, and objectives
2. An ambitious yet realistic plan
3. Time and money to plan, research problems and solutions, and conduct ongoing staff development and follow-up directly related to the planned changes
4. Organization of staff, parents, and community members into committees to ensure implementation by monitoring, problem solving, and evaluating the often challenging kinds of efforts necessary to accomplish significant changes in an organization

Evaluation in particular should address the progress of individual students at risk as well as provide group data desegregated by student population (e.g., the disadvantaged; limited-English-proficient students — both primary language and English-dominant; migrant students; and the handicapped). Data should be both qualitative and quantitative and include (1) students' risks of not succeeding; (2) success in learning the district's core curriculum; and (3) preparation for advancement to the next level of education or transition to work as applicable.

Students at Lathrop Intermediate School, Santa Ana Unified School District, proudly show off their art awards.

At Dos Palos Elementary School, four action teams focus on literacy, parent and community outreach, assessment, and leadership. Teachers report back to their school "families" on the activities of the action team.
(Far West Laboratory ESS Case Study, 1994)

SEVEN-STEP MODEL

The following seven-step model is based on the most current research-based School Improvement Program model of schoolwide change. It is significantly different from previous models of planning. For example, the plan that results from this process would:

◆ Be only a few pages in length (i.e., just enough to describe the school's major change efforts and not a description of everything going on at the school).

◆ Be based on a vision of desired outcomes (i.e., not just a mission or goals and objectives).

◆ Require the school to incorporate outside information on new, more effective practices as a basis for proposed changes.

Perhaps most significant is the component for implementing and evaluating what is planned through the ongoing monitoring and problem-solving of school-site committees.

This model is presented *both* as a means of generally upgrading the quality of the overall school program, as is its purpose in the School Improvement Program, *and* as a model of what the demonstration schools might do to focus *specifically* on how to put into practice the approach outlined in the previous section. The seven steps to this model of planning, implementing, and evaluating are as follows:

1. Establish *organizational structures* to carry out the planning for change.

2. Develop a *vision* for students at risk that is radically different from the status quo.

3. Investigate the *strengths and weaknesses* of the school's current core and supplementary services, including special education services, using an outside standard of comparison, such as the state program quality criteria; the state frameworks, handbooks, and curriculum guides; *Here They Come: Ready or Not, It's Elementary, Caught in the Middle, Second to None;* and so forth.

4. Identify and research program weaknesses or problems considered to be the most serious and which, if addressed, would result in *the biggest payoffs* in academic success for students at risk.

5. Develop and adopt a *limited number of change initiatives* (e.g., an enriched, thinking math curriculum; improved supplementary service coordination; increased access to social services for abused children; reform of screening, intervention, and assessment practices in special education; improved primary language services for LEP students for the most language-dependent parts of the curriculum; and increased parent involvement).

   The development of these change efforts should involve "outside information" on the most successful practices for addressing the identified problems and opportunities for the staff to interact intensely with it. This information can be brought into the school via staff development programs, reports on visits to exemplary programs, research articles, outside consultants, and so forth. Also to be considered is how to integrate these efforts with any others currently being addressed at the school. To process and make use of such new information, opportunities need to be made available to teachers, such as study groups, curriculum development groups, innovation monitoring committees, peer coaching, professional book clubs on campus, planning meetings, problem-solving meetings.

   Finally, how the school spends its available money to support its newly identified change efforts will likely need significant reorganization. First, all available budgets at a school site should be looked at comprehensively (i.e., as a lump sum). Next, on the basis of a review of local outcomes as well as a study of what research and exemplary practice suggests is most effective, money should no longer be spent on the status quo (i.e., good practices) but invested in new practices (i.e., better and best practices).

6. Initiate a *staff development* program — supported by time allotted for frequent collegial support, problem solving, and peer coaching. Everything should relate directly to the vision and the changes decided on by the school community as a result of its investigations into what works with the most challenging, vulnerable students.

7. Establish *organizational structures to monitor, adjust, and evaluate the implementation* of the change efforts. They might include new committees, work teams, or cadres; decision-making protocols and budget structure; language policies; and parent involvement opportunities.

All available budgets at a school site should be looked at comprehensively. Money should no longer be spent on the status quo (i.e., good practices) but invested in new practices, (i.e., better and best practices).

SCHOOL SITE STRUCTURES

Planning, implementation, and evaluation of significant change cannot be done without adequate school-site structures. In most cases these structures are configurations of *persons, time, and resources* to do the work necessary to change the way the school does business. Some suggested structures for these purposes are listed as follows:

1. *The School Site Council (SSC)*, where required, plans and guides the work of the Site Leadership Team and its committees, which plan, monitor, evaluate, and otherwise ensure the implementation of each change effort.

2. The *Site Leadership Team* is a key element in the School Improvement Program, Chapter 1 Program Improvement, the Achievement Council, and the Comer Model. It includes the principal and representative staff, who function as the major resources for the SSC to coordinate and monitor all planning, implementation, and evaluation activities. The Site Leadership Team should also include one person, such as a vice principal or resource teacher, charged with overseeing the daily implementation of the program.

3. *Student Study Team Plus (SST+)* is a mechanism to provide information for schoolwide planning, usually through the Site Leadership Team, related to trends or systemic problems discovered through working with individual students. This is the Mental Health Team in the Comer Model and the "plus" function of the SST+ as proposed in *California's Special Education Strategic Plan*. For implementation the team ensures that each student benefits maximally from school despite incidental problems that may arise.

4. *Staff committees* are assigned during planning to identify the school's strengths, weaknesses, and problems as well as to research causes and solutions or promising practices. After planning is completed, these committees would be reconfigured and assigned under the direction of the Site Leadership Team and SSC to ensure the implementation and evaluation of each change effort.

5. *A model of staff development* is needed that proceeds from theory to modeling to practice and feedback to coaching. It should be supplemented by periodic, group collegial support activities, debriefings, and problem-solving activities — all directly related to the development or implementation of the major change initiatives established by the school.

6. *Time* is set aside for meetings designed to:
   - ◆ Consider a new vision for students at risk.
   - ◆ Identify strengths, weaknesses, and problems in the current program relative to these students, using student outcome data as a principal starting point.
   - ◆ Research causes and solutions.
   - ◆ Finalize the major change efforts.
   - ◆ Establish a way to monitor and evaluate implementation.
   - ◆ Create a staff development program related to the change efforts.

After planning is complete and the change efforts are developed, time is arranged for monitoring or problem-solving meetings to ensure implementation of the change efforts, conduct staff development, and carry out the process and product evaluation.

ALLOCATION OF TIME AND FUNDING

How time can be set aside for planning, implementing, or evaluating will vary by school site and school district and involve overcoming each one's unique obstacles in a variety of ways. Schools and school districts in the state that have found creative methods to harness time for these purposes will be provided as models for the schools and districts that participate in the demonstration phase of ESS. Without sufficient time set aside for planning and implementing, however, no significant change in school culture or student success rates will occur, and staff may continue to be frustrated with overload at every turn.

Reform in the eighties was often compared with changing a flat tire while going 70 miles an hour on the freeway. The implication is that we have an impossible task because we are not given the time to stop driving and take care of our problems. Restructuring in the nineties, it could be argued, is worse. Now we are being asked not only to change the flat tire while continuing at 70 miles an hour but to reengineer the car at the same time.

Cross country team members in Santa Ana Unified School District warm up before practice.

As mentioned in the section on staff development, teachers in Japan and China spend more time at school each day than American teachers do but less time with students. These Asian teachers enjoy built-in time to prepare, collaborate, learn, polish lessons — in short, to reform or restructure their programs daily as they see fit. It is just such built-in time that American teachers so desperately need, especially those engaged in dramatically improving their school as a powerful learning organization for students most at risk.

Staff focus their time and efforts on students at Carver Elementary School, San Diego City Unified School District

One important source of time for change in California schools is *the eight staff development days* available to schools that opt for the school-based coordination program (SBCP). These are student-free days for which the school continues to receive its normal average daily attendance (ADA) monies. Although students do miss contact time with their teachers, a school can become significantly more effective for the diversity of challenging students enrolling today through the effective use of these days. In such cases, the seat time missed in class is well worth it. For serious and dramatic improvements, most schools with high percentages of students at risk will need all eight days each year for several years. One school has been so creative as to obtain a state waiver to divide up the eight days into 34 segments of one and one-half hours each throughout the school year for ongoing staff development and planning.

A second popular scheme is *to bank time.* That is, the school day is extended, say, 15 minutes per day for four days. Students then are released an hour early one day a week to give teachers planning and staff development time. The early release day is usually a day other than Monday or Friday, for obvious reasons. No student contact time is lost, and teachers have time to improve their effectiveness. Different versions of time banking exist (e.g., sometimes the accumulated time is taken biweekly rather than weekly). The Elementary Education Office, California Department of Education, has published a monograph describing these and other ideas on using time effectively. It is entitled *Finding Time for Change* (August, 1994).

Money to support staff time and other expenses related to planning, including the local review of the school's program, research into "a better way," staff development, implementation of new change efforts, and evaluation will likely need to be found in the funds currently available at the school or solicited from outside sources. The first step, consequently, is a reassessment of how spending is structured at the school and why and how this status quo will be changed to support the expenses of planning and eventually implementing changes in that status quo. "We have no money" cannot be an acceptable response. Rather, schools need to ask, "How could we spend our money more effectively in the short run? In the long run?"

Toward this end it may be helpful to use the school-based coordination program (SBCP) approach. This approach looks at the lump sum of a school's state categorical resources, including the School Improvement Program (SIP), Economic Impact Aid (EIA), State Compensatory Education, Limited-English-Proficient (LEP), and S.B. 1882 Staff Development funds. In addition, the school should examine all categorical funds, including Chapter 1, Chapter 2, Migrant, Title VII, lottery, and other federal, state, and private grants. Where legal obstacles to effective spending appear to exist, the Department will work with ESS demonstration schools and school districts to help them make the most efficient and effective use of their available monies without violating original legislative intent or diminishing services to specific groups of students.

A substantial rearrangement of spending will likely have to occur to support the kinds of curriculum, instruction, and categorical program reform advocated in the Every Student Succeeds initiative. The Department of Education has recommended that a school reserve approximately 30 percent of its School Improvement Program funds each year for supporting change rather than continuing to maintain the status quo. Instead of investing most of its funds in services provided by paraprofessionals and specialists, for example, a school may need to assign money for (1) staff development and follow-up; (2) the purchase of time for planning, implementing, assessment, and staff development and follow-up; (3) parent involvement; and (4) purchase of materials and equipment in accordance with the major reorganization or program reforms agreed on in the planned change efforts. In addition, some staff may need to be "multifunded" to make it easier to use their expertise more efficiently with any student who could benefit.

> *"We have no money" cannot be an acceptable response. Rather, schools need to ask, "How could we spend our money more effectively in the short run? In the long run?"*

Besides investing in human capital and building the capacity of the school as an effective organization, acquiring new materials can be a very high priority, especially with teachers being trained to conduct their classrooms in a manner radically different from the past. To do so requires building a school's supply of print and audiovisual materials both in classrooms and in a separate facility (including the cost of a librarian); buying literature to support the language arts (in English and other languages as necessary) and current materials in history-social science; acquiring computer hardware and software that is productive rather than merely skills-based; collecting manipulatives, models, and maps; and providing adequate equipment and consumable supplies for vocational programs, the visual and performing arts, and the sciences.

Financial support should also be considered for special programs for the cost of specialists, early childhood programs, before- and after-school programs, parenting and infant care programs, classes that expand or broaden the core curriculum, and parent and community involvement and training. The Department of Education will also determine what role it can play as a broker to help participating demonstration schools and districts cut costs by sharing services and research whenever possible.

As for the ESS initiative, an *evaluation format* has been developed by Far West Laboratory for collecting and analyzing qualitative and quantitative data on the participating schools' performance related to student populations, staff, administrators, parents, and the community.

Preferably, much of the same data will be collected in the same format as the data gathered and analyzed as their school did their initial planning. The format includes annual surveys, test data, the *School Performance Report*, periodic self-studies and program quality reviews, and coordinated compliance reviews to be reported to the staff, the school site council, the school district office and governing board, other feeder or receiving schools, parents, community, and the California Department of Education. ❦

6 WHATEVER ELSE IT TAKES

The focus of this element — within legal, professional, and ethical standards — is to ensure that everything is done to help every student in school be successful academically, psychologically, and socially. Each school context is unique, and distinctive variations on any model or practice may have to be developed for each student to be successful. At the same time, not everything is known that needs to be known to help all students become successful in school. Certainly, this framework does not include all the many good ideas and promising practices available to schools looking to make their program dramatically more successful for their lowest achievers. School-site educators may have to assume the role of detectives in finding or pioneers in developing new strategies, models, or structures that work for their students.

The success or failure of this initiative at a school site should not ultimately rest on the model or practices discussed. Given the present knowledge in this field and the work of committed educators on promising models such as Accelerated Schools, Success for All, and the Comer Model, what is described in this publication can serve as a useful sampler of what is likely to work best for students who are at risk of school failure. However, the school district, school, and community — including the Legislature and the California Department of Education — must see themselves ultimately as responsible for and capable of helping each student to become successful in school — no matter what!

It can be seen on street signs, on the town's water tower and on every piece of official city stationary. "Education First!" It is the motto of the entire city of Santa Ana — a powerful statement about the community's commitment to its schools. The Santa Ana District is the eighth largest district in the state. It has 44 schools and a 95 percent minority student population.

(continued on next page)

Santa Ana is one of the districts to be named an ESS Demonstration District with seven of its schools actively participating as demonstration sites. Its former superintendent, Rudy Castruita, believes his role in the restructuring initiative "is to encourage as many schools as possible to take part."

The district restructured itself into four clusters, each containing a high school, intermediate schools and the elementary feeder schools of each cluster. This change set up a collaborative forum for schools to engage in ongoing dialogue about integrating and articulating programs, K-12, and to become aware of issues they should be addressing.

Restructuring has been like "a breath of fresh air" to the schools, said Superintendent Castruita. Out of the process the board has supported such changes as block scheduling, all-day kindergarten classes, differentiated ways of instruction, revised district policy, administration regulations regarding site-based management, class size reductions in grades one and two, restructuring the core curriculum at the elementary level, school integrated teams, and schools within school at the intermediate level.

A major focus of district support is staff development. "Teachers were asking what they could do collectively to educate their culturally diverse, urban youth," said Castruita. The district responded by providing six teacher development release days as well as offering a student leadership forum for 250 students hosted at the community college during those days.

The collaborative model between the district office and the individual schools has brought exciting dividends. "Last year the student dropout rate decreased by 61 percent and over the last two years the number of students graduating increased by 13 percent," Castruita said. "There is tremendous excitement and rapport in the district. The teachers' association has supported all restructuring requests and through the restructuring process there has been a rejuvenation of ideas."

The former superintendent said, "While the greatest adjustment the school board had to make was giving autonomy to sites, this is monitored. We are risk takers in this district." Restructuring has been a powerful catalyst for change in Santa Ana. (ESS Update, March, 1994)

THE CHALLENGE

ESS

This approach or any other is unlikely to succeed with the most underachieving students without the commitment and assistance of the school district office, parents, the community, the county office, local institutions of higher education, and the California Department of Education. The major mechanisms will likely be a combination of both top-down and bottom-up leadership, commitment, and collaboration. Additional funds have been awarded to some ESS demonstration districts and schools through the Demonstration of Restructuring in Public Education Program (S.B. 1274 and Chapter 1556). Additional federal funds will be available to districts and schools for systemic reform under Goals 2000: The Educate America Act. It is also clear that each district and school will eventually develop its own distinct successful model based on unique local conditions and resources. What cannot vary across contexts, however, is the commitment to develop a critical mass of willing and able participants — in schools, district and county offices, homes, community agencies, universities, and businesses.

In the final analysis success for students at risk of school failure will be the product not necessarily of a program but of dedicated individuals, their talents, and their personalities. It is hoped that the Every Student Succeeds initiative will appeal to participants' sense of pioneering spirit and celebrity of membership in a unique

Students at Paramount Elementary School, Azusa Unified School District, proudly display awards.

venture to create models of success for students at risk. But perhaps most significant is the possibility that through this kind of comprehensive approach and coordinated effort, the education community can usher in a new era of educational success for virtually every student.

EVERY STUDENT SUCCEEDS

REFERENCES & APPENDICES

REFERENCES

Advisory Task Force on At-Risk Schools. *Identifying and improving at-risk schools.* (Monograph from the Office of Instructional Strategies). Sacramento: California Department of Education, June, 1989.

Archbald, D.A., and F.M. Newmann. *Beyond standardized testing: Assessing authentic academic achievement in the secondary school.* Reston, Va.: NASSP, 1988.

Association for Supervision and Curriculum Development. *Toward the thinking curriculum: Current cognitive research.* Alexandria, Va.: Association for Supervision and Curriculum Development, 1989.

Benard, B. *Fostering resiliency in kids: Protective factors in the family, school, and community.* Portland: Western Regional Center for Drug-Free School and Communities Northwest Regional Educational Laboratory, 1991.

Berliner, D.C., and U. Casanova. *Putting research to work in your school.* New York: Scholastic, Inc., 1993.

Berman, P., B. Gerritz, and L. Lambert. *Expanding minority access to math/science careers: An analysis of the Cooperative College Preparatory Program (Vol. I).* Berkeley: BW Associates, April, 1985.

Berman, P., and M.W. McLaughlin. *Federal programs supporting educational change. Vol. viii: Implementing and sustaining innovations.* Santa Monica: Rand Corp., May, 1978.

Berman, Weiler Associates. *Restructuring California education: A design for public education in the twenty-first century, recommendations to the California Business Roundtable* (summary). Berkeley: BW Associates, 1988.

Bloom, B.S. The search for methods of instruction as effective as one-to-one tutoring. *Educational Leadership* (May, 1974), 4-17.

Brown, J.S., Al Collins, and P. Duguid. Situated cognition and the culture of learning. *Educational Researcher,* Vol. 18, No. 1 (January-February, 1989), 32-42.

Brown, P.R., and K. Haycock. *Excellence for whom?* Oakland: The Achievement Council, 1984.

California Department of Education. *Agenda for the twenty-first century: A blueprint for K-12 education.* Sacramento: Author, 1987.

California Department of Education. *A question of thinking: A first look at students; performance on open-ended questions in mathematics.* Sacramento: Author, 1989.

California Department of Education. *Basic principles for the education of language-minority students: An overview.* Sacramento: Author, 1983.

California Department of Education. *Bilingual education handbook: Designing instruction for LEP students.* Sacramento: Author, 1990.

California Department of Education. *California education summit: Meeting the challenge - The schools respond - final report.* Sacramento: Author, 1990.

California Department of Education. *California plan for career-vocational education - Part one: policy directions.* Sacramento: Author, 1989.

California Department of Education. *Caught in the middle: Educational reform for young adolescents in California public schools.* Sacramento: Author, 1987

ESS

California Department of Education. *Effective language arts programs for Chapter 1 and Migrant Education students.* Sacramento: Author, 1989.

California Department of Education. *Effective practices in achieving compensatory education-funded schools (Vols. I & II).* Sacramento: Author, 1984, 1987.

California Department of Education. *English-language arts framework for California public schools.* Sacramento: Author, 1987.

California Department of Education. *Enrichment opportunities guide: A resource for teachers and students in math and science.* Sacramento: Author, 1988.

California Department of Education. *Fact Book, 1993-94: Handbook of Education Information.* Sacramento: 1994.

California Department of Education. *Foreign language framework for California public schools, kindergarten through grade twelve.* Sacramento: Author, 1989.

California Department of Education. *Here they come: Ready or not!* Sacramento: Author, 1988.

California Department of Education. *History-social science framework for California public schools, kindergarten through grade twelve.* Sacramento: Author, 1988.

California Department of Education. *Increasing the number of minority students taking the SAT and the ACT: Evaluation report on pilot projects funded by AB 2321.* Sacramento: Author, 1988.

California Department of Education. *Quality criteria for elementary schools/middle grades/high schools.* Sacramento: Author, 1989.

California Department of Education. *SAT scores by ethnicity: 1980-1993.* Sacramento: Author, 1993.

California Department of Education. *Schooling and Language Minority Students: A Theoretical Framework.* Evaluation, Dissemination, and Assessment Center, California State University, Los Angeles, 1981.

California Department of Education. *Science framework for California public schools, kindergarten through grade twelve.* Sacramento: Author, 1990.

California Department of Education. *Selected references for teaching English as a second language.* Sacramento: Author, 1986.

California Department of Education. (Ed.) *Studies on immersion education: A collection for United States educators.* Sacramento: Author, 1984.

California Department of Education. *Selected references for teaching English as a second language.* Sacramento: Author, 1986.

California Department of Education. *The changing history-social science curriculum: A booklet for parents.* Sacramento: Author, 1990.

California Department of Education. *The changing language arts curriculum: A booklet for parents.* Sacramento: Author, 1990.

California Department of Education. *The changing mathematics curriculum: A booklet for parents.* Sacramento: Author, 1989.

California Department of Education. *Visual and performing arts framework for California public schools, kindergarten through grade twelve.* Sacramento: Author, 1989.

California Joint Select Task Force on the Changing Family. *Families and adolescents: Dealing with today's realities.* Sacramento: Joint Publications Office, State Capitol, 1990.

California Task Force to Promote Self-Esteem and Personal and Social Responsibility. *Toward a state of esteem.* Sacramento: California State Department of Education, 1990.

Carnegie Council on Adolescent Development. *Turning points: Preparing American youth for the 21st century.* New York: Carnegie Council on Adolescent Development, 1989.

Chang, J. M. A school-home-community-based conceptualizaton of LEP students with learning disabilities: Implications from a Chinese-American study.In J. Gomez and O. Shjabak (Eds.). *The Proceedings of the Third Annual Research Symposium on Limited English Proficient sutdents' Issues: Focus on evaluation and measurement.* Vol. II. Washington, DC: United States Department of Education, Office of Bilingual Education and Language Minority Affairs, 1993, 693-717.

Chang, J. M., and G. Fung. *Literacy support across multiple sites: Experiences of Chinese American LEP children in inner cities.* Paper presented at the Annual meeting of American Educational Research Association (AERA). April 4-8, 1994, New Orleans, Louisiana, 1994.

Clay, M. *The early detection of reading difficulties* (3rd Ed.). Portsmouth, NH: Heinemann, 1985.

Clay, M.M. *An observation survey of early literacy achievement.* Portsmouth, NH: Heinemann, 1993.

Cohen, E.G. *Designing groupwork: Strategies for the heterogeneous classroom.* New York: Teachers College Press, 1986.

Comer, J.P. Educating poor minority children, *Scientific American* (November, 1988), 42-48.

Comer, J.P. *Empowering minority students.* Sacramento: California Association for Bilingual Education, 1989.

Conrad, D., and D. Hedin. School-based community service: What we know from research and theory. *Phi Delta Kappan* (June, 1991), 743-749.

Cuban, L. A fundamental puzzle of school reform. *Phi Delta Kappan* (January, 1988), 341-344.

Cummins, J. The role of primary language development in promoting educational success for language minority students. In California State Department of Education (Ed.), *Schooling and language minority students: A theoretical framework* (pp. 1-49). Los Angeles: Evaluation, Dissemination and Assessment Center, California State University, Los Angeles, 1981.

Cummins, J. Empowering minority students: A framework for instruction. *Harvard Educational Review,* Vol. 56, No. 1 (February, 1986), 18-36.

DeAvila, E., S.E. Duncan, and C. Navarrette. *Finding out/descubrimiento.* Northvale, NJ: Santillana Publishing Co., 1987.

Dawson, M.M. Beyond ability grouping: A review of the effectiveness of ability grouping and its alternatives. *School Psychology Review,* Vol. 16, No. 3 (1987), 348-369.

Deal, T.E. & A.A. Kennedy. *Corporate cultures: The rites and rituals of corporate life.* Reading, Mass.: Addison-Wesley Publishing Co., 1982.

de Bono, E. *The CoRT thinking program* (2nd Ed.). Chicago: Science Research Associates, 1987.

Duncan, S.E., and E.A. DeAvila. Bilingualism and cognition: Some recent findings. *NABE Journal,* No. 4 (1979), 15-50.

Dweck, C. Motivational processes affecting learning. *American Psychologist,* Vol. 41, No. 10 (1986), 1040-1048.

Dweck, C. S., and E. S. Elliot. Achievement motivation. In *Personality, and Social Development,* edited by E. M. Hetherington. (Vol. IV of *Handbook of Child Psychology,* edited by P. H. Mussen.) New York: Wiley 1983.

Epstein, J.L. (Guest Ed.). *Parents and schools* (Entire issue). *Educational Horizons,* Vol. 66, No. 2 (Winter, 1988).

Evaluation, Dissemination, and Assessment Center. (Ed.). *Beyond language: Social and cultural factors in schooling language minority students.* Los Angeles: California State University, Los Angeles, 1986.

Fallows, J. *More like us: Putting America's native strengths and traditional values to work to overcome the Asian challenge.* Boston: Houghton Mifflin, 1989.

Featherstone, H. (Ed.). Organizing classes by ability. *Harvard Education Letter* (July 1987), 1-4.

Franzen, A.M., and R.L. Allington. Every child's right: Literacy. *The Reading Teacher,* Vol. 45, No. 2 (October, 1991), 86-90.

Frymeir, J., and B. Gansneder. *The Phi Delta Kappa study of students at risk: Collaborating to do research.* Bloomington, Iowa: *Phi Delta Kappan,* 1989, 142-146.

Goldenberg, C. and Gallimore, R. (1991, November). Local knowledge, research knowledge, and educational change: A case study of early Spanish reading improvement. *Educational Researcher, 20* (8), 2-14.

Gall, M.D., et al. *Tools for learning: A guide to teaching study skills.* Alexandria, Va.: Association for Supervision and Curriculum Development, 1990.

Gardner, H. *Frames of mind: The theory of multiple intelligences.* New York: Basic Books, 1983.

Gardner, H. *Multiple Intelligences: The theory in practice.* New York: Basic Books, 1993.

General Accounting Office. *Regulatory flexibility in schools: What happens when schools are allowed to change the rules?* (GAO/HEHS-94-102). Gaithersburg, Md.: U.S. General Accounting Office, April, 1994.

Genesee, F. *Learning through two languages: Studies of immersion and bilingual education.* Cambridge, Mass.: Newbury House, 1987. Good, T.L., and J.E. Brophy. *Looking in classrooms* (2nd Ed.). New York: Harper & Row, 1978.

Goldenberg, C., and R. Gallimore. Local knowledge, research knowledge and educational change: A case study of early Spanish reading improvement. *Educational Researcher,* Vol. 20, No. 8, (November, 1991), 2-14

Gonzales, P.C. *Equity and access in a language arts program for all students.* Sacramento: California Department of Education, 1988.

Good, T.L., and J.E. Brophy. *Looking in classrooms* (2nd Ed.). New York: Harper & Row, 1978.

Goodlad, J.I. *A place called school: Prospects for the future.* New York: McGraw-Hill, 1984.

Goodlad, J.I., and P. Keating. (Eds.). *Access to knowledge: An agenda for our nation's schools.* New York: College Entrance Examination Board, 1990.

Gorham, J. Assessment, classification and implications of learning styles in instructional interactions. *Communication Education,* Vol. 35, No. 4 (October, 1986), 411-417.

Guild, P.B. *Marching to different drummers.* Alexandria, Va.: Association for Supervision and Curriculum Development, 1985.

Guthrie, L.F., G.P. Guthrie, S. van Heusden, and R. Burns. *Principles of successful Chapter 1 programs: A guidebook for rural educators.* San Francisco: Far West Laboratory, 1989.

Hakuta, K., and L.J. Gould. Synthesis of research on bilingual education. *Educational Leadership* (March, 1987), 38-45.

Haycock, K., and S. Navarro. *Unfinished business: Fulfilling our children's promise.* Oakland: The Achievement Council, 1988.

Hord, S.M., W.L. Rutherford, L. Huling-Austin, and G.E. Hall. *Taking charge of change.* Alexandria, Va.: Association for Supervision and Curriculum Development, 1987.

Howard, J. The Efficacy Seminar for Educators. Boston: The Efficacy Institute, 1993.

Jacobs, H.H. *Interdisciplinary curriculum: Design and implementation.* Alexandria, Va.: Association for Supervision and Curriculum Development, 1989.

Jenkins, J.R., C. G. Pious, and M. Jewell. Special education and the regular education initiative: Basic assumptions. *Exceptional Children,* Vol. 56, No. 6 (1990), 479-491.

Johnson, D.W., and R.T. Johnson. *Learning together and alone: Cooperative, competitive, and individualistic learning.* Englewood Cliffs, NJ: Prentice-Hall, 1987.

Johnson, D.W., R.T. Johnson, and E.J. Holubec. *Circles of learning: Cooperation in the classroom.* Edina, Minn.: Interaction Book Company, 1986.

Johnson, P.W. Teacher-conducted brown bag lunch seminars: One solution to staff development in isolated schools. *Journal of Staff Development,* Vol. 10, No. 2 (Spring, 1989), 42-43.

Joyce, B. (Ed.). *Changing school culture through staff development.* Alexandria, Va.: Association for Supervision and Curriculum Development, 1990.

Joyce, B., and B. Showers. The coaching of teaching. *Educational Leadership,* Vol. 40, No. 1 (October, 1982), 4-10.

Joyce, B., and B. Showers. *Student achievement through staff development.* New York: Longman, 1988.

Joyce, B., and M. Weil. *Models of teaching.* Englewood Cliffs, NJ: Prentice Hall, 1972.

Kagan, S. *Cooperative learning: Resources for teachers.* Riverside: University of California, 1985.

Kantrowitz, B., and P. Wingert. How kids learn. *Newsweek,* April 17, 1989, 50-57.

Keefe, J.W. (Ed.). *Profiling and utilizing learning style.* Reston: National Association of Secondary School Principals, 1988.

Kelley, B. A movement at hand. *California Tomorrow* (Spring, 1988), 27-32.

Kerman, S., T. Kimball, and M. Martin. *Teacher expectations and student achievement: Coordinator manual.* Los Angeles: Office of the Los Angeles County Superintendent of Schools, 1980.

Kimbrough, J., and P.T. Hill. *Problems of implementing multiple categorical education programs.* Santa Monica: Rand, September, 1983.

Kirst, M., et al. *Conditions of Children in California.* Policy Analysis for Coherent Education (PACE), Berkeley: School of Education, University of California, Berkeley, 1989.

Knapp, M.S., and P.M. Shields (Ed.). *Better schooling for the children of poverty: Alternatives to conventional wisdom* (Vols. 1-2). Washington, D.C.: U.S. Department of Education, Office of Planning, Budget & Evaluation, 1990.

Kohn, A. *No contest: The case against competition.* Boston: Houghton Mifflin, 1986.

Kozol, J. *Savage inequalities: Children in America's schools.* New York: Crown Publishing, 1991.

Krashen, S., and D. Biber. *On course: Bilingual education's success on California.* Sacramento: California Association for Bilingual Education, 1988.

Levin, H.M., Glass, G.V., and Meister, G.R. *The cost-effectiveness of four educational interventions.* Stanford, CA: Stanford University. Institute for Research on Educational Finance and Governance. (ERIC Document Reproduction Service No. ED 246 533) 1984.

Levin, H.M., R. Polkinghorn, and D.M. Bartels. *Accelerated Schools: The inquiry process and the prospects for school change.* Boston: Paper presented at the annual meeting of the American Educational Research Association, April, 1990.

Levien, M., and R. Trachtman (Eds.). *American Business and the public school: Case studies of corporate involvement in public education* New York: Teachers College Press, 1988.

Long, M.H., and P. A. Porter. Group work, interlanguage talk and second language acquisition. *TESOL Quarterly,* Vol. 19, No. 2, 1985, 207-228.

Lyons, C. A. Reading recovery: An effective intervention program that can prevent mislabeling children as learning disabled. In *ERS Research Digest,* 1990, 17-23.

McLaughlin, M.W., and P.M. Shields. Involving low-income parents in the schools: A role for policy? *Phi Delta Kappan* (October, 1987), 156-160.

McLaughlin, M.W., and D.D. Marsh. Staff development and school change. *Teachers College Record,* Vol. 80, No. 1 (September, 1978), 69-94.

Means, B., and M.S. Knapp (Eds.). *Teaching advanced skills to educationally disadvantaged students.* Washington, D.C.: U.S. Government Printing Office, March, 1991.

Nai-Lin Chang, H. *Newcomer programs: Innovative efforts to meet the educational challenges of immigrant students.* San Francisco: California Tomorrow, 1990.

National Education Association. *Academic tracking: Report of the NEA Executive Committee Subcommittee on Academic Tracking.* Washington, D.C.: National Education Association, Instruction and Professional Development, July, 1990.

National Research Council, Mathematical Sciences Education Board. *Reshaping school mathematics: A philosophy and framework for curriculum.* Washington, D.C.: National Academy Press, 1990.

Oakes, J. *Keeping track: How schools structure inequality.* New Haven: Yale University Press, 1985.

Ogbu, J.U. Research currents: Cultural-ecological influences on minority school learning. *Language Arts,* Vol. 62, No. 8 (December, 1985), 860-869.

Olsen, L. *Push out, step out: A report on California's public school dropouts.* Oakland: Citizen's Policy Center, 1982.

Olsen, L. *Crossing the schoolhouse border: Immigrant students and the California public schools.* San Francisco: California Tomorrow, 1988.

Olsen, L. *Bridges: Promising programs for the education of immigrant children.* San Francisco: California Tomorrow, 1989.

Olsen, L., et al. (1990). *Embracing Diversity: Teachers' voices from California's classrooms.* San Francisco: California Tomorrow, 1990.

Palincsar, A.S., and A.L. Brown. Reciprocal teaching of comprehension-fostering and comprehension-monitoring activities. *Cognition and Instruction,* Vol. 1, No. 2 (1984), 117-175.

Parkay, F.W., and S.B. Damico. Empowering teachers for change through faculty-driven school improvement. *Journal of Staff Development,* Vol. 10, No. 2 (Spring, 1989), 8-14.

Peale, E., and W.E. Lambert. The relation of bilingualism to intelligence. *Psychological Monographs* 76 (27, Whole No. 546), 1962.

Peterson, P.L., L.C. Wilkinson, and M. Hallinan. (Eds.). *The social context of instruction: Group organization and group processes.* New York: Academic Press, 1984.

Philliber, S. *Teen outreach: Program and outcome, 1984-1994*. Philliber Research Associates, NY, 1994.

Pinnell, G.S., M.D. Fried, and R.M. Estice. Reading recovery: Learning how to make a difference. *The Reading Teacher* (January, 1990), 282-295.

Posner, M.I. (Ed.). *Foundations of cognitive science*. Cambridge, Mass.: The MIT Press, 1989.

Psacharopoulos, G. (Ed.). *Economics of education: Research and studies*. New York: Pergamon Press, 1987.

Quality Education for Minorities Project. *Education that works: An action plan for the education of minorities*. Cambridge, Mass.: Massachusetts Institute of Technology, 1990.

Radius, M., and P. Lesniak. *Student study teams: A resource manual for trainers and implementors* (Rev. Ed.) Sacramento: California Department of Education, Special Education Division, 1988.

Ramirez, J. D., S. D. Yuen, and D. R. Ramey. *Executive summary: Evaluation report of the longitudinal study of structured English immersion strategy, early-exit and late-exit transitional bilingual education programs for language minority children*. San Mateo: Aguirre International, 1991.

Rekrut, M.D. (1994, February). Peer and cross-age tutoring: The lessons of research. *Journal of Reading, 37* (5), 356-352.

Resnick, L.B. *Education and learning to think*. Washington, D.C.: National Academy Press, 1987.

Resnick, L.B., and L.E. Klopfer. (Eds.). *Toward the thinking curriculum: Current cognitive research*. Alexandria, Va.: Association for Supervision and Curriculum Development, 1989.

Resnick, L.B. *Education and learning to think*. Washington, D.C.: National Academy Press, 1987.

Rich, D. *Megaskills in school and in life — the best gift you can give your child*. Boston: Houghton Mifflin, 1992.

Routman, R. *Transitions: From literature to literacy*. Portsmouth, NH: Heinemann, 1988.

Schaps, E., and D. Solomon. Schools and classrooms as caring communities. *Educational Leadership*, Vol. 48, No. 3 (November, 1990), 38-42.

Shields, P.M., E.D. Jay, T. Parrish, and C. Padilla. *Alternative programs and strategies for serving students with learning disabilities and other learning problems: Executive Summary*. Menlo Park: SRI International, 1989.

Slavin, R.E., N.L. Karweit, and N.A. Madden. *Effective programs for students at risk*. Boston: Allyn and Bacon, 1989.

Slavin, R.E. *Cooperative learning*. New York: Longman, 1983.

Slavin, R., S. Sharan, S. Kagan, R. Hertz-Lazarowitz, C. Webb, and R. Schmuck (Eds.). *Learning to cooperating, cooperating to learn*. New York: Plenum Press, 1985.

Slavin, R.E. Ability grouping and student achievement in elementary schools: A best-evidence synthesis. *Review of Educational Research,* Vol. 57, No. 3 (Fall, 1987), 293-336.

Slavin, R.E. Synthesis of research on grouping in elementary and secondary schools, *Educational Leadership* (September, 1988), 67-77.

Slavin, R. E., N. L. Karweit, and B. A. Wasik. *Preventing early school failure: Research, policy, and practice.* Boston: Allyn and Bacon, 1994.

Smith, F. *Joining the literacy club. Further essays into education.* Portsmouth, N. H.: Heinemann, 1988.

Stauffer, R. *The language-experience approach to the teaching of reading.* New York: Harper and Row, 1970.

Steinberg, A. (Ed.). When kids do science. *Harvard Education Letter* (May/June, 1990), 1-5.

Stevenson, H.W., and J.W. Stigler. *The learning gap: Why our schools are failing and what we can learn from Japanese and Chinese education.* New York: Summit Books, 1992.

University of California Task Force on Black Student Eligibility. *Making the future different.* Berkeley: University of California, 1990.

U.S. Department of Education. *Effective compensatory education sourcebook: Project profiles* (Vols. II-IV). Washington, D. C.: Superintendent of Documents, U.S. Government Printing Office, 1986-88.

U.S. Department of Education. *Final Report of the National Assessment of the Chapter 1 Program.* Washington, D.C.: U.S. Department of Education, February, 1993.

U.S. Department of Education. *What works: Schools that work - Educating disadvantaged children.* Washington, D.C.: U.S. Department of Education, 1988.

Weinstein, C.F., and R.F. Mayer. The teaching of learning strategies. In M.C. Wittrock (Ed.), *Handbook of Research on Teaching* (3rd Ed.) (pp. 315-327). New York: Macmillan, 1986.

Wells, C. G. *The meaning makers: Children learning language and using language to learn.* Portsmouth, N.H.: Heinemann, 1986.

Wells, C. G., and G. L. Chang-Wells. *Constructing knowledge together: Classrooms as centers of inquiry and literacy.* Portsmouth , N. H.: Heinemann, 1992.

Willig, A.C. A meta-analysis of selected studies on the effectiveness of bilingual education. *Review of Educational Research,* Vol 55, No. 3 (1985), 269-317.

Winget, P., & J. Kirk. California's special education exemplary programs: 1988-89. Sacramento: Resources in Special Education (RiSE), 1989.

Wittrock, M.C. (Ed.). *Handbook of research on teaching* (3rd ed.). New York: Macmillan, 1986.

Wood, G.H. *Schools that work: America's most innovative public education programs.* New York: Dutton, 1992.

The Young & Rubicam Foundation. *The one place: A new role for American schools.* New York: St. Martin's Press, 1991.

ESS

EVERY STUDENT SUCCEEDS

APPENDIX A
ESS DEMONSTRATION DISTRICTS AND SCHOOLS
ESS INITIATIVE NETWORK 1994-95

Alisal Union Elementary School District

Robert R. Flores, Acting Superintendent
Jeanne Herrick, ESS Contact
1205 East Market St.
Salinas, CA 93905-2899
408/753-5700
Fax: 408/753-5709

Alisal Community

William Deeb, Principal
1437 Del Monte Ave.
Salinas, CA 93905
408/753-5720
Fax: 408/753-5725
Approximately 950 students are enrolled, 600 of whom are LEP (61%). 42% are on AFDC with 90% participating in the Free Lunch Program. 88% of the students participate in the Compensatory Education Program. The school has Chapter 1, Chapter 2, the School Improvement Program, the State Compensatory Program, and Bilingual funds as supplementary to the regular funds.

Virginia Rocca Barton

Robert Caraveo, Principal
680 Las Casitas Dr.
Salinas, CA 93905
408/753-5770
Fax: 408/753-5797
Approximately 1,000 students are enrolled, 687 of whom are LEP (67%). 31% are on AFDC with 85% participating in the Free Lunch Program. The school has an S.B. 1274 demonstration restructuring grant. 84% of the students participate in the Compensatory Education Program. Supplemental funding sources are Chapter 1, Chapter 2, Miller-Unruh, and the School Improvement Program.

Frank Paul Elementary School

Anastacio Cabral, Principal
1300 Rider Ave.
Salinas, CA 93905
408/753-5740
Fax: 408/753-5268
Approximately 750 students are enrolled, 582 of whom are LEP (74%). 27% are on AFDC with 92% participating in the Compensatory Education Program. The school has an S.B. 1274 restructuring demonstration grant. Supplemental funding sources are Chapter 1, Chapter 2, Miller-Unruh, and the School Improvement Program.

Sanborn Elementary

Ruben Pulido, Principal
901 North Sanborn Rd.
Salinas, CA 93905
408/753-5760
Approximately 740 students are enrolled, 550 of whom are LEP. 32% are on AFDC with 94% participating in the Free Lunch Program. 100% of students participate in the Compensatory Education Program. The school has an S.B. 1274 demonstration restructuring grant. Supplemental funding sources are Chapter 1, Chapter 2, Miller-Unruh, and the School Improvement Program.

Azusa Unified School District

Rod Gaeta, Superintendent
Nancy Moore, ESS Contact
546 South Citrus Ave.
Azusa, CA 91702
818/967-6211
Fax: 818/339-5592

Azusa High School

Joe Garcia, Principal
240 North Cerritos Ave.
Azusa, CA 91702
818/969-3010
Approximately 1,400 students are enrolled. The student ethnicity count is 58% Hispanic, 34% white, and 4% Black. 16% of these students are on AFDC and 34% participate in the Free Lunch Program. The school has a 5% dropout rate. Supplemental funding sources are the State Compensatory Education Program, the State Bilingual Program, and Grade 10 Counseling.

Henry Dalton Elementary School

Sharon Lindsay, Principal
500 East Tenth St.
Azusa, CA 91702
818/969-7901
Approximately 360 students are enrolled, 140 of whom are LEP (38%). 32% are on AFDC with 75% participating in the Free Lunch Program. 55% of students participate in the Compensatory Education Program. The school has an S.B. 1274 restructuring demonstration grant. Supplementary funding sources are Chapter 1, the State Compensatory Education Program, and the School Improvement Program.

Ellington Elementary School
Carolyn Wertz, Principal
5034 North Clydebank
Covina, CA 91722
818/915-6434
Approximately 410 students are enrolled, 11% of whom are LEP. 17% are on AFDC with 47% participating in the Free Lunch Program. Supplemental funding sources are the State Bilingual Program and the School Improvement Program.

Foothill Middle School
Robert Ware, Principal
151 North Fenimore Ave.
Azusa, CA 91702
818/334-0619
Approximately 781 students are enrolled, 26% of whom are LEP. 22.8% are on AFDC with 63.6% participating in the Free Lunch Program. Supplemental funding sources are the School Improvement Program and the State Bilingual Program.

Gladstone Street Elementary School
Cynthia Cervantes McGuire, Principal
1040 East Gladstone St.
Azusa, CA 91702
818/915-6441
Approximately 490 students are enrolled, 27% of whom are LEP. 18% are on AFDC with 63% participating in the Free Lunch Program. 30% of the students participate in the Compensatory Education Program. Supplemental funding sources are Chapter 1, the State Bilingual Program, and the School Improvement Program.

Gladstone High School
Albert Webb, Principal
1340 North Enid
Covina, CA 91722
818/334-0419
Approximately 1,450 students are enrolled, 307 of whom are LEP (21%). 13% are on AFDC with 31% participating in the Free Lunch Program. The student ethnicity count is 69% Hispanic, 20% white, 3% Filipino, and 3% Black. The school has a very low dropout rate. Supplemental funding source is the State Bilingual Education Program.

Hodge Elementary School
Arturo Delgado, Principal
700 West 11th St.
Azusa, CA 91702
818/334-5189
Approximately 430 students are enrolled, 32% of whom are LEP. 15% are on AFDC with 56% participating in the Free Lunch Program. 48% of the students participate in the Compensatory Education Program. Supplemental funding sources are Chapter 1, the State Bilingual Program, and the School Improvement Program.

Charles H. Lee Elementary School
Joe Peake, Principal
550 North Cerritos Ave.
Azusa, CA 91702
818/969-9781
Approximately 550 students are enrolled, 250 of whom are LEP (46%). 28% are on AFDC with 88% participating in the Free Lunch Program and the Compensatory Education Program. Supplemental funding sources are Chapter 1, the State Bilingual Education, and the School Improvement Program. The school also has an S.B. 1274 School Restructuring grant.

Longfellow Elementary School
Mimi Zamary, Principal
245 West Tenth St.
Azusa, CA 91702
818/969-3011
Approximately 350 students are enrolled, 44% of whom are LEP. 33% are on AFDC with 66% participating in the Free Lunch Program. 59% of the students participate in the Compensatory Education Program. Supplemental funding sources are Chapter 1, State Bilingual Program, and the School Improvement Program.

Magnolia Elementary School
Susan Waller-Mummert, Principal
945 East Nearfield
Azusa, CA 91702
818/969-9695
Approximately 510 students are enrolled, 17% of whom are LEP. 13% are on AFDC with 43% participating in the Free Lunch Program. Supplemental funding sources are the State Bilingual Program and the School Improvement Program.

Mountain View Elementary School
Bettina Hunt, Principal
201 North Vernon
Azusa, CA 91702
818/969-7943
Approximately 400 students are enrolled, 160 of whom are LEP (39%). 20% are on AFDC with 73% participating in the Free Lunch Program. 50% of the students are participating in the Compensatory Education Program. Supplemental funding sources are Chapter 1, the State Bilingual Program, and the School Improvement Program.

Murray Elementary School
Burke Hamilton, Principal
505 East Renwick Rd.
Azusa, CA 91702
818/334-8204
Approximately 643 students are enrolled, 58% of whom are LEP. 31% are on AFDC with 81% participating in the Free Lunch Program. 58% of the students participate in the Compensatory Education Program. Supplemental funding sources are Chapter 1, the State Bilingual Program, and the School Improvement Program.

Paramount Elementary School
Adele McCready, Principal
409 West Paramount Ave.
Azusa, CA 91702
818/969-9729
Approximately 690 students are enrolled, 260 of whom are LEP (39%). 50% of the students are participating in the Compensatory Education Program. The supplementary funding sources are Chapter 1, the State Bilingual Program, and the School Improvement Program.

W.R. Powell Elementary School
Lee Ann Baker-Dunne, Principal
1035 East Mauna Loa
Azusa, CA 91702
818/969-9785
Approximately 400 students are enrolled, 80% of whom are LEP (19%). 24% are on AFDC with 62% participating in the Free Lunch Program. 31% are participating in the Compensatory Education Program. Supplemental funding sources are Chapter 1, the State Bilingual Program, and the School Improvement Program.

Valleydale Elementary School
Corey James, Principal
700 South Lark Ellen
Azusa, CA 91702
818/334-0357
Approximately 483 students are enrolled, 40% of whom are LEP. 13% are on AFDC with 69% participating in the Free Lunch Program. 53% are participating in the Compensatory Education Program. Supplemental funding sources are Chapter 1, the State Bilingual Program, and the School Improvement Program.

Dos Palos Oro-Loma Joint Unified School District

Ed Butler, Superintendent
Max Harrell, ESS Contact
2041 Almond St.
Dos Palos, CA 93620
209/392-6101
Fax: 209/392-3347

Bryant Middle School
Brian Walker, Principal
c/o Dos Palos Oro-Loma Joint Unified School District
2041 Almond St.
Dos Palos, CA 93620
209/392-6186
Fax: 209/392-2636
Approximately 690 students are enrolled, 11% of whom are LEP. 30% of the students are on AFDC with 74% participating in the Free Lunch Program. 37% are Compensatory Education participants. Supplemental funding sources are Chapter 1, the State Compensatory Education, the State Bilingual Program, Chapter 2, and the School Improvement Program.

George Christian Kindergarten
Gayle Bonds, Principal
c/o Dos Palos Oro-Loma School District
2041 Almond St.
Dos Palos, CA 93620
209/392-2766
Fax: 209/392-3347
Approximately 167 students are enrolled in this kindergarten-only school. 31% of students are LEP. 29% are on AFDC, 74% participate in the Free Lunch Program, 65% are participating in the Compensatory Education Program. Supplemental funding sources are

Chapter 1, the State Compensatory Education Program, Chapter 2, and the School Improvement Program.

Dos Palos High School
Tom Scheidt, Principal
1701 East Blossom St.
Dos Palos, CA 93620
209/392-2131
Fax: 209/392-2705
Approximately 695 students are enrolled, 22% of whom are LEP. 20% are on AFDC with 62% participating in the Free Lunch Program. 38% of the students are participating in the Compensatory Education Program. Supplemental funding sources are Chapter 1, the State Bilingual Program, Grade 10 Counseling, and the School Improvement Program.

Dos Palos Elementary School
Gayle Bonds, Principal
2149 Almond St.
Dos Palos, CA 93620
209/392-2151
Fax: 209/392-3347
Approximately 790 students are enrolled, 27% of whom are LEP. 30% of students are on AFDC with 74% participating in the Free Lunch Program. 66% of all students are participating in the Compensatory Education Program. Supplemental funding sources are Chapter 1, the State Bilingual Program, State Compensatory Education, Miller-Unruh, Chapter 2, and the School Improvement Program. The school also has an S.B. 1274 School Restructuring grant.

Oro Loma Elementary School
Anita Damiano, Principal
5609 North Russell Ave.
Firebaugh, CA 93622-9526
209/364-6116
Fax: 209/364-6322
Approximately 215 students are enrolled, 27% of whom are LEP. 14% of the students are on AFDC with 79% participating in the Free Lunch Program. 84% are participating in the Compensatory Program. Supplemental funding sources are Chapter 1, State Compensatory Education, the State Bilingual Education Program, Miller-Unruh, Chapter 2, and the School Improvement Program.

Fontana Unified School District
Karen Harshman, Superintendent & ESS Contact
9680 Citrus Ave.
Fontana, CA 92335-5594
909/357-5000
Fax: 909/355-3034

Almeria Middle School
Richard Roth, Principal
7723 Almeria Ave.
Fontana, CA 92335
909/357-5350
Fax: 909/357-5360
Approximately 1,359 students are enrolled, 16% of whom are LEP. 21% are on AFDC with 38% participating in the Free Lunch Program. 47% are participating in the Compensatory Education Program. The school has an S.B. 1274 restructuring demonstration grant. Supplemental funding sources are Chapter 1 and the State Bilingual Program.

Fontana High School
Kay Rager, Principal
9453 Citrus Ave.
Fontana, CA 92335-5595
909/357-5500
Fax: 909/357-5629
Approximately 4,243 students are enrolled, 10% of whom are LEP. 12% are on AFDC with 9% participating in the Free Lunch Program. The ethnic count at this high school is 51% Hispanic, 37% white and 8% Black. Dropout rate is low at 6.8%. Supplemental sources are Chapter 1, the State Bilingual Program, Grade 10 Counseling, and Chapter 2. The school also has an S.B. 1274 School Restructuring grant.

West Randall Elementary School
Carolyn Kezsley, Principal
15620 Randall Ave.
Fontana, CA 92335-4499
909/357-5780
Approximately 853 students are enrolled, 30% of whom are LEP. 19% are on AFDC with 64% participating in the Free Lunch Program. The school has an S.B. 1274 restructuring demonstration grant. 57% of the students participate in the Compensatory Education Program. Supplemental funding sources are Chapter 1, the State Bilingual Program, Miller-Unruh, Chapter 2, and the School Improvement Program.

Southridge Middle School
Gary Soto, Principal
14500 Live Oak
Fontana, CA 92335-2873
909/357-5420
Fax: 909/822-4609
Approximately 1,195 students are enrolled, 13% of whom are LEP. 11% are on AFDC with 25% participating in the Free Lunch Program. The ethnic count at this school is 50% Hispanic, 35% white and 10% Black. Supplemental funding sources are the State Bilingual Program, Chapter 2, and the School Improvement Program.

Hayward Unified School District
Marlin Foxworth, Superintendent & ESS Contact
24411 Amador St.
Hayward, CA 94540-5000
510/784-2600
Fax: 510/782-7213

Glassbrook Elementary School
Gina Gonzalez, Principal
975 Schafer Rd.
Hayward, CA 94544
510/783-2577
Approximately 455 students are enrolled, 50% of whom are LEP. 36% are on AFDC with 91% participating in the Free Lunch Program. 100% of the students are participating in the Compensatory Education Program. Supplemental funding sources are Chapter 1, the State Bilingual Program, and the School Improvement Program.

Shepherd Elementary School
Kip Anderson, Principal
27211 Tyrrell Ave.
Hayward, CA 94544
510/783-1182
Approximately 423 students are enrolled, 37% of whom are LEP. 43% are on AFDC with 92% participating in the Free Lunch Program. 100% of the students are participating in the Compensatory Education Program. The school has an S.B. 1274 restructuring demonstration grant. Supplemental funding sources are Chapter 1, the State Bilingual Program, and the School Improvement Program.

Tennyson High School
Gordon Pipkin, Principal
27035 Whitman Rd.
Hayward, CA 94544
510/582-0707
Fax: 510/582-0964
Approximately 1,256 students are enrolled, 33% of whom are LEP. 40% are on AFDC with 44% participating in the Free Lunch Program. 28% of the students are participating in the Compensatory Education Program. Dropout rate is about 8%. Student ethnic count is 12% Asian, 35% Hispanic, 21% white, 18% Black, 8% Filipino, and 4% Pacific Islander. Supplemental funding sources are Chapter 1, the State Bilingual Program, and Grade 10 Counseling.

Tyrrell Elementary School
Sandra Rogers-Hare, Principal
27000 Tyrrell Ave.
Hayward, CA 94544
510/783-2936
Approximately 607 students are enrolled, 39% of whom are LEP. 51% are on AFDC with 78% participating in the Free Lunch Program. The school has an S.B. 1274 restructuring demonstration grant. Supplemental funding sources are Chapter 1, the State Bilingual Program, and the School Improvement Program.

La Vista Intermediate School
Marcos Guerrero, Principal
27845 Whitman St.
Hayward, CA 94544
510/538-5905
Approximately 584 students are enrolled, 23% of whom are LEP. 28% are on AFDC with 42% participating in the Free Lunch Program. Supplemental funding sources are Chapter 1, the State Bilingual Program, and the School Improvement Program.

Long Beach Unified School District

Dr. Carl A. Cohn, Superintendent
Steve Fish, ESS Contact
701 Locust Ave.
Long Beach, CA 90813
310/436-9931
Fax: 310/435-4056

Millikan High School

Margie Godfrey, Principal
2800 Snowden Ave.
Long Beach, CA 90815
310/425-7441
Fax: 310/425-1151
Approximately 3,574 students are enrolled, 30% of whom are LEP. 12% are on AFDC with 48% participating in the Free Lunch Program. Dropout rate is 17% schoolwide with the highest dropout rate being among Blacks at 25% and Hispanics at 23%. Ethnic count is 40% Hispanic, 28% white, 12% Black, and 12% Asian. Supplemental funding sources are the State Bilingual Program and Grade 10 Counseling.

Riley Elementary School

Laurie Inman, Principal
3319 Sandwood St.
Lakewood, CA 90712
310/420-9595
Fax: 310/496-1176
Approximately 740 students are enrolled, 43% of whom are LEP. 32% are on AFDC with 73% participating in the Free Lunch Program. 55% of the students are participating in the Compensatory Education Program. Supplemental funding sources are Chapter 1, State Compensatory Education, and the School Improvement Program.

Pajaro Valley Unified School District

Anthony Avina, Superintendent
Bert Post, ESS Contact
165 Blackburn St.
Watsonville, CA 95077
408/728-6230
Fax: 408/761-6010

Alianza Elementary School

Michael Jones, Principal
440 Arthur Rd.
Watsonville, CA 95076
408/728-6333
Approximately 558 students are enrolled, 73% of whom are LEP. 15% are on AFDC with 73% participating in the Free Lunch Program. 73% of the students are participating in the Compensatory Education Program. Supplemental funding sources are Chapter 1, the School Improvement Program, the State Bilingual Program, and Chapter 2.

E.A. Hall Middle School

Murray Schekman, Principal
2201 Brewington
Watsonville, CA 95076
408/728-6270
Approximately 1,170 students are enrolled, 54% of whom are LEP. 16% are on AFDC with 36% participating in the Free Lunch Program. Supplemental funding sources are the School Improvement Program, the State Bilingual Program, and Chapter 2.

Renaissance High School

Cathryn Hatch, Principal
11 Spring Valley Rd.
La Selva Beach, CA 95076
408/728-6344
Fax: 408/728-6419
Approximately 220 students are enrolled, 37% of whom are LEP. 13% are on AFDC with 49% participating in the Free Lunch Program. Supplemental funding source is the State Bilingual Program. The school also has an S.B. 1274 School Restructuring grant.

Starlight Elementary School
Georgia Grijalva, Principal
225 Hammer Dr.
Watsonville, CA 95076
408/728-6979
Approximately 699 students are enrolled, 56% of whom are LEP. 21% are on AFDC with 71% participating in the Free Lunch Program. 58% of the students are participating in the Compensatory Education Program. Supplemental funding sources are Chapter 1, the School Improvement Program, and the State Bilingual Program. The school also has an S.B. 1274 School Restructuring grant.

Watsonville High School
Lorraine Sandoval, Principal
250 East Beach St.
Watsonville, CA 95076
408/728-6390
Fax: 408/761-6013
Approximately 2,216 students are enrolled, 38% of whom are LEP. 9% are on AFDC with 24% participating in the Free Lunch Program. Supplemental funding sources are the State Bilingual Program, Grade 10 Counseling, and the Chapter 2 Program.

Sacramento City Unified School District
Dr. Terry Grier, Superintendent
Lily Keyser, ESS Contact
1619 N St.
Sacramento, CA 95812
916/264-4300
Fax: 916/264-4191

Fern Bacon Middle School
Raymond Valdez, Principal
4140 Cuny Ave.
Sacramento, CA 95823
916/433-5000
Approximately 924 students are enrolled, 21% of whom are LEP, 9% are on AFDC with 62% participating in the Free Lunch Program. 50% of the students are participating in the Compensatory Education Program. The major ethnic groups at this school are Asian 26%, white 24%, Black 23%, and Hispanic 22%. Supplemental funding sources are Chapter 1, the State Bilingual Program, Chapter 2, and the School Improvement Program.

San Diego City Unified School District
Dr. Bertha O. Pendleton, Superintendent
4100 Normal St.
San Diego, CA 92103
619/293-8686
Fax: 619/293-8267

Carver Elementary School
Wilma Kozai, Principal
3251 Juanita St.
San Diego, CA 92105
619/583-7021
Approximately 488 students are enrolled, 40% of whom are LEP. 40% are on AFDC with 69% of the students participating in the Free Lunch Program. 100% of the students are participating in the Compensatory Education Program. Supplemental funding sources are Chapter 1, the State Bilingual Program, Chapter 2, and the School Improvement Program.

Santa Ana Unifed School District
Don Champlin, Acting Superintendent
Linda DelGuidice, ESS Contact
1405 French St.
Santa Ana, CA 92701
714/558-5501
Fax: 714/558-5802

Gerald P. Carr Intermediate
Vincent Tafolla, Principal
2120 West Edinger St.
Santa Ana, CA 92704
714/241-6430
Approximately 1,685 students are enrolled, 70% of whom are LEP. 9% of students are on AFDC with 72% participating in the Free Lunch Program. Major ethnic groups at the school are Hispanic 91% and Asian 5%. 35% of the students are participating in the Compensatory Education Program. Supplemental funding sources are Chapter 1, the State Bilingual Program, and the School Improvement Program.

Century High School
Thomas Reasin, Principal
1401 South Grand
Santa Ana, CA 92705
714/568-7000
Fax: 714/568-7038
Approximately 2,388 students are enrolled, 50% of whom are LEP. 10% are on AFDC with 38% participating in the Free Lunch Program. 11% of the students participate in the Compensatory Education Program. Major ethnic groups are Hispanic 87% and Asian at 6%. Dropout rate for the school is low at 7%. Supplemental funding sources are Chapter 1, the State Bilingual Program, and Grade 10 Counseling.

Benjamin Franklin Elementary School
Linda Genis, Principal
210 West Cubbon
Santa Ana, CA 92701
714/558-5684
Approximately 664 students are enrolled, 90% of whom are LEP. 13% of students are on AFDC with 90% participating in the Free Lunch Program. 100% of the students are participating in the Compensatory Education Program. Supplemental funding sources are Chapter 1, the State Bilingual Program, and the School Improvement Program.

Lathrop Intermediate
Greg Rankin, Principal
1111 South Broadway
Santa Ana, CA 92707
714/558-5701
Approximately 1,897 students are enrolled, 76% of whom are LEP. 12% are on AFDC with 87% participating in the Free Lunch Program. Major ethnic groups are Hispanic 94% and Asian at 4%. Supplemental funding sources are Chapter 1, the State Bilingual Program, and the School Improvement Program.

Saddleback High School
Marylouise Ortega, Principal
2802 South Flower St.
Santa Ana, CA 92707
714/513-2900
Fax: 714/513-2911
Approximately 2,873 students are enrolled, 39% of whom are LEP. 8% are on AFDC with 28% participating in the Free Lunch Program. Dropout rate at the school is a low 6%. Major ethnic groups are Hispanic 68%, Asian 15%, and White at 12%. Supplemental funding sources are the State Bilingual Program and Grade 10 Counseling.

William Spurgeon Intermediate
Marilyn Maher, Principal
2701 West Fifth St.
Santa Ana, CA 92703
714/558-5586
Fax: 714/558-5527
Approximately 1,428 students are enrolled, 68% of whom are LEP. 13% of students are on AFDC with 75% participating in the Free Lunch Program. 19% of the students are participating in the Compensatory Education Program. Major ethnic groups are Hispanic 91% and Asian 6%. Supplemental funding sources are Chapter 1, the State Bilingual Program, and the School Improvement Program. The school also has an S.B. 1274 School Restructuring grant.

Adeline Walker Elementary School
Robert DeBerry, Principal
811 East Bishop
Santa Ana, CA 92701
714/558-5685
Approximately 700 students are enrolled, 84% of whom are LEP. 19% are on AFDC with 82% participating in the Free Lunch Program. 31% of the students participate in the Compensatory Education Program. Supplemental funding sources are Chapter 1, the State Bilingual Program, Chapter 2, and the School Improvement Program.

APPENDIX B
ESS NETWORK MEETINGS

There have been five ESS networking meetings held for all staff of participating districts and schools.

These three-day meetings were held in Ontario during November, 1991; in San Diego during March, 1992; in Monterey during October, 1992; in Long Beach in March, 1994; and in Orange County during October, 1994.

All of the past ESS meetings have focused on networking with other ESS districts and schools through school visitations, actively listening to presentations from requested speakers, and participation in job-alike and grade level-alike activities.

"PLANNING FOR EVERY STUDENT'S SUCCESS"

The first training, "Planning for Every Student's Success," utilized the trainer of trainer techniques that could be used in schools to discuss broad issues from a variety of specific perspectives. Restructuring stories involving the Azusa and Fontana Unified School Districts were told, led by their superintendents, Duane Stiff and Anthony Lardieri, respectively. These districts shared their restructuring efforts with the group and fielded question from the audience. Districts networked by clusters to share information about schools and districts, identifying the challenges, stating problems, and generating solutions.

"MAKING SUBSTANTIVE CHANGES FOR EVERY STUDENT'S SUCCESS"

During the second ESS networking meeting, entitled "Making Substantive Changes for Every Student's Success," participants learned from Henry Levin, founder of the Accelerated Schools Network, about the Accelerated Schools Experience and lessons on school change. This meeting was held just prior to the submission of applications for S.B. 1274 demonstration grant awards; therefore, a portion of the meeting was utilized to help schools prepare their competitive grant applications. The San Diego City Unified School District, led by Deputy Superintendent Bertha Pendleton, gave a presentation of their restructuring efforts. School visits were the highlight of this meeting giving the visitors a look into San Diego schools and the work of San Diego teachers and students.

"EVERY STUDENT SUCCEEDS: WHAT IS STUDENT SUCCESS?"

The third networking meeting, entitled "Every Student Succeeds: What is Student Success?" offered a framework for change and restructuring, thus creating equity in education for each student. This framework was provided by keynote speaker Jeff Howard of The Efficacy Institute, Lexington, Massachusetts. This presentation created heated debate around race, ethnicity, and class. The participants learned examples of how to integrate all core and supplementary services for each student including services provided by categorical programs through examples and presentations by Superintendents Merrill Grant of Pajaro Valley Unified School District and Robert Flores of Alisal Union Elementary School District. Schools and district staff were introduced to two task force reports: *Second to None: The High School Task Force Report*, and *It's Elementary: the Elementary Grades Task Force Report*. School visits were again a highlight of the conference, with participants enjoying seeing activities inside Alisal Elementary School District and Pajaro Unified School Districts schools, classrooms, and students and teachers at work.

"NETWORKING, EQUITY, AND ACCOUNTABILITY"

The fourth networking meeting continued to network through school site visitations, sharing and debating school change issues by elementary, middle grades, and high school levels. Sessions were presented by The Efficacy Institute to help participants understand the consequences of efficacy attitudes (i.e., the belief that every student can succeed) in teachers and the effects of teachers' sense of efficacy on students, other teachers, and other aspects of the school environment.

A large part of the conference was dedicated to assessment strategies, which included sessions on the restructuring schools protocol for examining student work for what matters most, learning the potential of performance assessment from the California Assessment Collaborative, led by Catherine Jamentz, Director, and examining the essential elements of portfolio samples of student work. School visitations to Long Beach Unified School District, Azusa Unified School District, Santa Ana Unified School District, and networking among elementary and middle grade participants were again a highlight for the conference participants. Outstanding ESS leadership awards were presented to Karin Polacheck, board member from Long Beach Unified School District, and Rudy

Castruita, Superintendent of Santa Ana Unified School District. Also, Carl Cohn, Superintendent of Long Beach Unified School District addressed the attendees and explained how ESS was being utilized as an important philosophy in his district.

"ACCOUNTABILITY"

The fifth networking meeting addressed the accountability issues for the success of students at risk of school failure. The participating school/district teams, consisting of four to seven members worked together to produce a plan that would define content and performance standards for mathematics and early and/or adult literacy. Additionally, various assessment strategies were selected to measure the performance of each student (e.g., portfolio assessment rubrics, performance-based assessments) to include all students, especially limited-English-proficient students, special education and economically deprived students and other students at risk of school failure.

The first day of the meeting was led by guest speaker Bill Honig, Superintendent of Public Instruction from 1982 to 1993. The general session was dedicated to learning about the content focus: mathematics and early adult literacy. Presentations were made on the interactive mathematics program, college preparatory mathematics, early literacy, Project Reach, and adult literacy during the morning sessions. Assessment strategies to measure student performance sessions consisted of presentations on portfolio assessments for high school mathematics; the *California Learning Record,* by Mary Barr; assessment strategies for adult literacy, by Patricia Rickard; and program quality review, a strategy for analyzing student work by the entire school staff. The second day and half of the third day were utilized by the school/district teams to develop their plans for defining content and performance standards as well as selecting assessment strategies to measure student performance. This staff development session was putting into practice the philosophy of allowing time for school staff to plan, develop, and implement powerful instructional strategies for successful student learning. The group gathered together for two hours at the end of the third day to share, network, and summarize their group work. Outstanding ESS leadership awards were presented to Rod Gaeta, Superintendent of the Azusa Unified School District, and to Robert Flores, retired Superintendent of the Alisal Union Elementary School District.

ESS

Appendix C
RESOURCES

STATE/NATIONAL PROGRAMS	LOCAL MODELS

ACCELERATED SCHOOLS

Stanford University
Department of Education
Accelerated Schools Project
Professor Henry Levin
Stanford, CA 94305
415/725-1676

Burnett Academy
San Jose Unified School District
850 N. Second Street
San Jose, CA 95112
408/998-6267

BILINGUAL EDUCATION

Bilingual Case Studies Model
Two-Way Immersion Programs
California Department of Education
Office of Bilingual Education
721 Capitol Mall, 2nd Floor
Sacramento, CA 95814
David Dolson, Consultant
916/657-3938

Bilingual Preschool Program
Carpenteria Unified School District
Robert H. Keatinge
Director, Special Projects
1400 Linden Avenue
Carpinteria, CA 93013
805/684-4511

Two-Way Bilingual Model
River Glen Elementary School
San Jose Unified School District
1610 Bird Avenue
San Jose, CA
408/998-6240

COMPENSATORY EDUCATION

California Department of Education
721 Capitol Mall, 2nd Floor
Sacramento, CA 95814
Hanna Walker, Manager
916/657-2527

John Davidson School
Vallejo City Unified School District
436 Del Sur Street
Vallejo, CA 94591
707/556-8430

EVEN START

U.S. Department of Education
Elementary and Secondary Programs
Compensatory Education
600 Independence S.W.
Room 4400/Portals
Washington, DC 20202-6132
202/260-4021

California Department of Education
Compensatory Education
721 Capitol Mall, 2nd Floor
Sacramento, CA 95814
Sallie Wilson, Consultant
916/657-3825

Chula Vista Elementary School
District (5 yr. Grantee)
84 East J Street
Chula Vista, CA 91910
619/425-2362

Healdsburg Union School
District (6 yr. Grantee)
565 Damas Lane
Healdsburg, Ca 95448
707/431-3470

STATE/NATIONAL PROGRAMS	LOCAL MODELS

READING RECOVERY

California State University,
San Bernardino
Department of Education
5500 University Parkway
San Bernardino, CA 92407
Stan Swartz, California Director
909/880-5646

Alisal Union Elementary
School District
1205 East Market Street
Salinas, CA
408/753-5700

STANDARD ENGLISH PROFICIENCY

California Department of Education
Office of Compensatory Education
721 Capitol Mall, 2nd Floor
Sacramento, CA 95814
916/657-2527
Yvonne Strozier

Vallejo City Unified School District
Special Projects Office
211 Valle Vista LAvenue
Vallejo, CA 94590
707/644-8921

SUCCESS FOR ALL

Center for Child Development
Johns Hopkins University
3505 North Charles Street
Baltimore, MD 21218
Robert Slavin, Director
410/516-0370

El Vista Elementary School
Modesto City Elementary
School District
450 El Vista Avenue
Modesto, CA
209/576-4665

STATE/NATIONAL PROGRAMS

ADVANCEMENT VIA INDIVIDUAL DETERMINATION (AVID)

San Diego County Office of Education
6401 Linda Vista Road
San Diego, CA 92111
619/292-3500

GENDER/ETHNIC EXPECTATIONS OF STUDENT ACHIEVEMENT (GEESA)

Graymill
8450 Hickman Road, Suite 29
Des Moines, IA 90325
515/252-8650

TEACHER EXPECTATION AND STUDENT ACHIEVEMENT (TESA)

Los Angeles County Office of Education
9300 Imperial Highway
Downey, CA 90242
Elsa Brizzi, TESA Coordinator
310/922-6167

ADDITIONAL RESOURCES

Benjamin E. Mays Institute
236 Auburn Avenue
Atlanta, GA 30303
404/223-6297

Central Park East
Secondary School
1573 Madison Avenue
New York, NY 10029
212/860-8935
founded by Debbie Meier

Far West Laboratory for
Educational Research and
Development
730 Harrison Street
San Francisco, CA 94107-1242
415/565-3000

High/Scope
600 North River Street
Ypsilanti, MI 48197
313/485-2000

Prosocial Development Program
for Children
Developmental Study Center
Eric Schaps, Director
2000 Embarcadero, Suite 305
Oakland, CA 94606-5300

Resources in Special
Education (RiSE)
650 Howe Avenue, Suite 300
Sacramento, CA 95825
800/894-9799

Santa Fe Indian School
1501 Cerrillo Road
P.O. Box 5340
Santa Fe, NM 87502

Teen Outreach Program
Sponsored by
the Junior League
Suzanne Henderson,
State Coordinator
7840 Madison Avenue, Suite 185
Fair Oaks, CA 95628
916/961-5549

ESS

EVERY STUDENT SUCCEEDS